THE PRINCIPLES OF
OBJECTIVE TESTING IN GEOGRAPHY

THE PRINCIPLES OF OBJECTIVE TESTING SERIES

General Editor: Douglas M. McIntosh
C.B.E., LL.D., M.A., B.SC., M.ED., PH.D., F.R.S.E., F.E.I.S.
Principal, Moray House College of Education

THE PRINCIPLES OF

Objective Testing in Geography

RAYMOND B. SALMON
Moray House College of Education

THOMAS H. MASTERTON
Moray House College of Education

HEINEMANN EDUCATIONAL BOOKS
LONDON AND EDINBURGH

Heinemann Educational Books Ltd

LONDON EDINBURGH MELBOURNE TORONTO
AUCKLAND JOHANNESBURG SINGAPORE
IBADAN NAIROBI HONG KONG NEW DELHI

ISBN 0 435 35700 X

First published 1974

Published by Heinemann Educational Books Ltd
48 Charles Street, London WIX 8AH

Printed in Great Britain by
Morrison & Gibb Ltd., Edinburgh

Preface

In recent years, criticism of the examination system has become widespread. In particular the reliability of the traditional forms has been called in question. For this reason, new types of examination have been devised. Of these, the so-called 'objective' type has been almost universally accepted in North America, and is being increasingly used in Britain. The construction of good objective-type examinations requires a considerable amount of skill in framing the questions and in composing the test as a whole. Moreover, individual subjects use different types of material, attach varying degrees of importance to different objectives, and have different problems. It is to assist teachers of Geography to construct and use objective-type tests that this book has been produced.

Contents

List of Plates

Between pages 66 and 67

1. *The Purposes of Examinations*

Measurement and evaluation are essential in education. Some assessment of achievement must be made regularly in order to establish whether a pupil has mastered the course of study on which he is engaged and is capable of proceeding to the next stage. An estimate of a pupil's potential ability is also necessary.

To be effective, the teacher must be able to define (in terms of human behaviour) the objectives of that part of the curriculum which is being taught; objectives should be clearly defined so that the extent to which they are being attained may be assessed throughout the course. A variety of measuring instruments should be used by the teacher in making assessments. Tests and examinations should be supported by oral questioning, and exercises and practical work should all be used in assessing both the pupil's ability and achievement. Objective testing is a most useful tool for this purpose.

USES OF TESTING

Examining or testing has two major purposes: (1) as an instrument of assessment, and (2) as a teaching instrument.

1. *As an instrument of assessment*—used in this way it fulfils the purposes:

(a) to measure the level of achievement;
(b) to predict future attainment;
(c) to select between candidates.

2. *As a teaching instrument*—for this purpose it can:

(a) reveal the extent to which teaching has succeeded or failed;
(b) provide motivation for both teacher and pupil.

1. *As an Instrument of Assessment*

(a) *Achievement*

Both the objectives of the course of study and the standards of achievement expected must be clearly defined so that the pupils are given some indication of the nature of the objectives and the standards which they are expected to attain. Such standards may be fixed subjectively by the teacher or a group of teachers who establish a syllabus or scheme of work. If standards are to be determined objectively the test has to be set to a large sample of pupils who have studied the course. Standardized tests are those which have been used on a fairly large sample of the population and the norms provided with the tests indicate standards for different ages or levels of ability.

Many external examinations indicate the results by awarding a pass or fail and make no effort to distinguish between candidates in the two categories: a pupil who just passes is given the same certificate as one who scores a very high mark. Many external examination boards, however, have introduced a grading system, which enables authorities to discriminate between candidates.

(b) *Prediction*

Many of the examinations at the end of secondary schooling are used to predict the success with which a pupil will engage in a course of higher education. Normally such examinations have not been specifically constructed with this purpose in mind as they were originally intended to mark the successful completion of secondary education. With the increasing variety of higher education, the pass/fail method of issuing results makes predication more difficult and has led to the demand for finer gradings.

(c) *Selection*

Examinations are frequently used to select a number of pupils for admission to a particular course of study. Selection may be of two kinds. First, when the purpose of the examination is to ensure that pupils who are chosen have the ability and the educational attainment which will enable them to undertake a further course. In such instances, the examination is of the qualifying type and all those who reach the specific standard are considered fit to proceed. Generally such examinations are of the pass/fail type. Secondly, when the number of candidates to be selected is determined before the examination or test is set. It is assumed that the examination can make the fine distinction between candidates on the borderline. The smaller the number of candidates to be selected, the more accurate the measuring instrument has to be.

Examinations which serve one of these two purposes are normally constructed in a different manner. In the first instance, the examination does not need to distinguish between candidates near the top of the distribution of marks, and in the second case there is no need to separate those near the bottom of the distribution. The important principle to be observed is that the examination or test should be constructed according to the purposes which it has to fulfil.

2. Examinations as a Teaching Instrument

(a) The effectiveness of teaching

External examinations are used to produce marks and once these have been issued no further consideration is given to what has been written by the pupil. In school, examinations or tests of some nature should be a necessary feature of classroom work. These should not be formal examinations but tests to check whether the learning experiences created by the teacher have been effective. Such tests should have built into them a diagnostic function as it is important for the teacher to discover what the pupil does not know and cannot do as well as establishing what he does know and can do. If a high proportion of the class is unable to answer a specific question, the teacher must inquire into the teaching method used for this topic.

(b) Motivation

The knowledge that a specific standard has to be achieved by a certain time gives purpose to teaching and learning. Teachers will work hard to ensure that their pupils who are striving to gain admission to university are proficient in the work of the examination syllabus, and the pupils have a clearly defined goal which channels their energies. Motivation has been shown to be a most important factor in learning, and a very important teaching skill is the motivation of pupils to maximum effort.

MULTIPURPOSE EXAMINATIONS

One of the weaknesses of examination results is that they are often used for a variety of purposes. Examinations at the end of the secondary school are used for entrance qualifications to many different professions which use these examinations simply because they are available. If the various professions were to set their own entrance examinations the schools would find difficulty in preparing pupils for a very wide range of examinations with varying syllabuses. National external examinations such as the SCE in Scotland and the GCE in England and Wales are used for entrance qualifications for many courses in higher education. They were once mainly used for university entrance but are now used by many different types of institutions.

EXAMINATION AND TEST RESULTS

Generally, examination or test results are expressed as a total of the marks obtained for each question although a pupil's total performance may not be of the first importance. For example, in a test used for diagnosis it is the pupil's failures on specific questions which have to be studied, and similarly where the test is used as a teaching instrument the pupil's success in individual questions may point to the effectiveness of the teacher in specific areas of the course of study or it may point to deficiencies in the pupil's learning.

The results of tests can be expressed by: (1) numerical marks, (2) categoric marks, (3) rank orders.

1. *Numerical Marks*

(a) *Raw score*

The total performance of a pupil is generally signified by a numerical mark. In an objective test, as one mark is generally awarded to each correct answer, the total number of correct answers is the total score. The sum of the marks obtained for each question is termed a raw score and by itself is of little significance even when the total number of questions is also given: the average marks of a class must at least be known in order to indicate the level of difficulty of the test.

(b) *Standard score*

A mark has significance only when it is related to the marks of a fairly large number of pupils of the same age or at the same stage in a course of study. Sixty may indicate a good performance or a poor one, depending upon the achievement of other pupils who have sat the test. For example, if the average mark is 45, then 60 is an above average score but if the average is 70 then the same mark represents a below average performance.

Even knowledge of the average mark is insufficient to give full meaning to a mark since in some cases the scores will be spread over a wide range whereas in others the range may be a narrow one. Mathematics tests generally give a wide scatter of marks but in subjects such as art the range may be restricted. When scores from different tests are added, the subjects which have a wide range of marks have greater discriminatory value than those which provide a relatively small scatter around the average mark. Marks can be made to have equal weight by making the scatters the same. The scatter of marks may be expressed by the standard deviation,* and a standard score is the distance of a mark from the mean or average of the marks in terms of standard deviation.

$$S = \frac{X - M}{\sigma_2}$$

where X is the raw score, M is the mean mark, σ_2 the standard deviation and S the standard score.

(c) *Percentage mark*

For a long while, the percentage mark has been used as a means of expressing the results of examinations, with 50 per cent being regarded as a pass mark and anything below it regarded as failing. This of course is quite an arbitrary decision.

The main use of this method of expressing results is to enable different sets of marks to be compared. For example, it is convenient to express as percentages a score of 38 out of 50 in arithmetic and 42 out of 60 in mathematics, in order to compare performances.

* See D. M. McIntosh, *Statistics for the Teacher* (Pergamon, 1967), page 38.

(d) *Percentile*

Another method of expressing a score in relation to other marks is to express it as a percentile, that is the mark below which a specified percentage of marks fall. For example, $P75 = 62$ indicates that 75 per cent of the marks fall below 62; or, the 75th percentile is 62.

2. *Categoric Marks*

A pupil's total score may be placed in a category. The usual way of describing marks by this method is by an A, B, C, D, E classification. Categories of this nature have to be defined and a generally adopted technique is to divide the marks into groups of 5, 20, 50; 20, and 5 per cent of the total group: categoric mark A includes top 5 per cent of the marks. A less precise definition of the five categories is, 'well above average', 'above average', 'average', 'below average', 'well below average'.

3. *Rank Order*

Arranging marks in order of merit is another method of relating a pupil's achievement to that of the others who have been tested. Rank 1 is given to the pupil with the highest score and the subsequent ranks are allocated according to the pupil's place in the order of merit. When several pupils have the same score the ranks are averaged and each pupil given the same rank. For example, if the 4th, 5th, 6th and 7th pupils have the same score each is awarded a rank 5·5. Similarly, identical scores for pupils who are placed 8th, 9th and 10th in order of merit result in each being awarded the rank of 9.

A rank indicates the level of performances of a pupil only in relation to the other pupils sitting the test. If the ability level of the group is low, a rank of 5 may indicate a low level of achievement.

NORMS

When a test is for a specific age group following a clearly defined syllabus, it is possible by setting the test to a fairly large representative sample of pupils to establish standards of achievement.

The simplest method of providing norms is to construct a table giving the percentile or categoric marks for a given score and age. For example, the achievement of a pupil of the age of 16 years 2 months who scores 32 on a specific standardized test can be interpreted by reading from a table the percentile or category into which the pupil falls. Standardized tests of this nature must be very carefully constructed.

There are then several methods of expressing the results of a test but their intended use will determine, to a large extent, the one chosen.

2. *Purposes of Geography Examinations*

Why do teachers of geography set tests? Their prime purpose is to measure their pupils' present level of achievement in order to:
- (a) diagnose defects and identify strengths in their teaching and the pupils' learning;
- (b) try to forecast how their pupils will perform later in their school life or in their careers;
- (c) discriminate among their pupils, produce an 'order of merit'.

They may also set tests in order to:
- (a) make pupils work harder, to stimulate effort;
- (b) to maintain standards, their pupils' and their own.

Tests and examinations are set at various intervals. The purpose of the test is the main factor in determining frequency. Diagnostic tests may be used as frequently as once a month, whereas external examinations may only be encountered by a pupil once or twice in his school career.

A DIAGNOSTIC DEVICE AND TEACHING INSTRUMENT

First the class teacher may use a test as a diagnostic device. He may wish to find out the state of his pupils' factual knowledge, their ability to comprehend geographical situations and to apply certain acquired skills. He will then use the results of his inquiry to indicate defects in such knowledge and ability, and later attempt to remedy these defects.

To be most useful and relevant to the teaching and learning situation of normal classroom work, such a test should be set by one teacher, to one class, on a specific range of facts or skills, directly after work on these facts or skills has taken place. For example, a teacher introduces a class to the nature and construction of isarithm maps. He shows the construction of a contour map by interpolation of isarithms between a number of spot heights. He supervises class exercises of a similar type, giving further explanation and help to individual pupils. Afterwards he tests the pupils' grasp of the techniques involved by setting another interpolation exercise as a test. (See page 83 for an example of this.) From a study of the resulting maps he finds that certain pupils do not yet understand the nature of the cartographic skills involved. The teacher is now in a position to give further explanation where it is most needed, and if necessary recast his method of teaching those skills. Furthermore, from the results of the test he can find out which pupils have fully assimilated the skills and have applied them carefully in the new situation. These pupils can then be passed on to a further stage in the work. He will also find those pupils who evidently understand the technique but have not exercised a desirable degree of care in the interpolation of the isarithms. The teacher may then point out this deficiency.

It is best for such classroom diagnoses to take place frequently, not just at the end of a term or a session. They can be arranged whenever suitable after a particular piece of work—after the study of industry in Japan, after work on latitude and longitude as a reference system, after a visit to a local factory. It is also best for these tests to take place informally with no special preparations, no foreknowledge of the event. There should be no sense of foreboding, no feeling that the tests are obstacles to be overcome. Pupils must understand that the tests are used to help the teacher help them.

The results of such diagnostic tests should of course be entered in the pupils' records, but the creation of a record of attainment is not the prime purpose. These tests are instruments for use by the teacher in his day-to-day routine, so that he may recognize where some pupils may need more help, spur able pupils on to greater achievement, and be helped to compare his 'teaching output' with the 'learning input' of his pupils, and indeed increase his efficiency in the classroom.

Such tests are of direct benefit to the pupils. Children need to know what a teacher expects of them. Frequent informal classroom tests help them to find out.

FOR SELECTION AND PROGNOSIS

Why else might a geography teacher set a test? He may be told by his headmaster to produce a graded list of his pupils. This will be used for discrimination purposes; pupils will be compared with one another. The headmaster may wish to use the present achievements of the pupils as a basis for forecasting short-term school performance. This will help him solve an administrative problem and allow him to break down a large class or group of pupils into small, fairly homogeneous groups. For example, at the end of the second year in a secondary school, and on an estimate based on second-year performance, he may allocate some pupils to a course of advanced studies, leading to a higher certificate, some to less advanced certificate work and others to a less academic course of study, a non-certificate group.

In order to produce some kind of estimate of his pupils' present level of achievement, the class teacher may set a special examination—a 'promotion' examination. Otherwise he may rely on his continuous assessment of the pupils' work over the entire session. When he has the necessary information he must present it in such a way that pupils are easily compared with one another.

He may use a list of percentages. Such statistics by themselves may not be very helpful and the teacher should supplement them with an interpretive key, for example:

Over 80 per cent excellent
70 to 80 per cent very good
60 to 69 per cent good
40 to 59 per cent fair
30 to 39 per cent poor
Less than 30 per cent is very poor

Such categorization would usually be affected by the teacher's own judgement of the difficulty of the test, by his standard of marking and also by the abilities of the pupils. In another situation 70 per cent might be an excellent mark, in yet another 50 per cent might be remarkably poor.

Many teachers find a system of alphabetical categories sufficient for this purpose. Pupils may be categorized as A, B, C, D or E. Again an explanatory verbal key may be needed when dealing with uninitiated parents, A being 'very good' and E being 'very poor'.

External Examinations

The main purpose of the external examination is forecasting; being the recognition and selection of that small section of any particular age group with ability to cope with further education, vocational training or a particular job. They are therefore hurdles, normally set at preconceived standards by groups of officials, and only attempted after work on officially published or approved syllabuses.

Class teachers are involved in that they first prepare their pupils along the lines laid down in the syllabus and then set and mark simulation examinations. Many teachers are also involved in setting, marking and moderating external examinations and may also be involved in matters of policy.

RAISING STANDARDS
AND PROVIDING MOTIVATION

Some teachers use tests for the purpose of trying to raise and maintain certain standards. They use an imminent test as a stimulus to work, to competitiveness—as a carrot. This aim *may* be partially attained when it is made known that the test result will be included in a school report.

The orienteering 'course' is an example of a competitive situation. Map reading standards must be high, map reading must be fast and accurate, compass work must be precise, and physical fitness is a prerequisite if the pupil is to have a chance of scoring well—or winning.

COMBINED PURPOSE TEST

One test may have many purposes. Reference to simulated external examinations will illustrate this. A simulation examination run by a class teacher will have *four purposes*, if it is to be used to full advantage:

1. Used as a teaching instrument it will give essential *practice*. Every candidate for a formal external examination needs experience and help in making difficult selections from a range of questions, in timing his answers, in conforming to acceptable examination hall routine.
2. It will be *diagnostic*. A simulation test will enable the class teacher to identify faults in a pupil's presentation and subject knowledge, and leave him to rectify these before the final external examination.

3. It will help the school to *forecast* a pupil's possible performance, and may indeed be used by a headmaster to dissuade pupil from committing himself to the external examinatio at that stage in his school career. In providing evidence ability, it may also influence the forecast given by th external examination.

4. A 'dummy run' is also a device for *stimulating effort*. Here w must of course assume that the candidate has a desire t succeed.

CONCLUSION

The class teacher may therefore use three main types of test:

1. The classroom test—short, immediate, informal. The prin cipal purpose will be diagnostic but results may be used i formulating continuous assessment.

2. The termly or sessional test, most commonly used for selec tion and prognosis, but other purposes should not be absent

3. The simulated external examination—referred to above.

In any test the geography teacher searches for evidence of th pupil's present achievement and tries to measure the level of tha achievement. He may use the results of the test to diagnose defects He may use them to discriminate among his pupils. He may us them to forecast possible future performance. He should alway try to use them with some scepticism, with healthy doubts abou their total accuracy and worth.

3. *Educational Objectives of Examinations*

Whenever an attempt is made to construct an examination, it is always essential to ask 'What are we trying to find out?' This is of crucial importance when examinations are being considered, because the answers to such a question define not only the objectives of the examinations, but in large measure also the objectives of education itself.

If it is agreed that the basic purpose of examination is to measure, then the question of what is being measured must be answered. Examinations and tests attempt to measure the success of the educational process or learning experience which the pupils have undergone, and this can be measured by determining what attainments and skills are now possessed by the pupils in each of the subjects they have studied. Naturally, attainments and skills vary from subject to subject, but it is possible to classify in general terms the kinds of attainments that are common to all subjects, and to list these in a logical sequence starting from the least intellectually demanding, such as simple recall, and proceeding to the more complex forms of intellectual activity such as analysis or evaluation. Educational objectives have been categorized as belonging to Cognitive, Affective and Psychomotor domains. This book deals with the first of these.

Educational objectives in the cognitive field were considered by a series of conferences held in the United States between 1949 and 1953. The conclusions of these discussions were edited by B. S. Bloom and published as *Taxonomy of Educational Objectives* in 1956. The objectives in the taxonomy are classified under six major headings:

1. Knowledge
2. Comprehension
3. Application
4. Analysis
5. Synthesis
6. Evaluation.

If this classification is accepted, it follows that a valid examination should seek to test and measure ability in several or all of these fields. It is of course possible that the educational goals for younger pupils will not include the more intellectually demanding of these objectives.

THE EXAMINATION AS A MEANS OF MEASURING KNOWLEDGE

A frequent criticism of examinations is that they merely measure knowledge—often equated with 'facts', and that the ability to remember facts is not a very good indicator of general ability or intelligence. Moreover, this emphasis on factual knowledge encourages rote learning and unimaginative teaching, and therefore distorts and impoverishes the whole educational process.

One reason why knowledge plays such an important role in educational teaching and testing is, of course, that the imparting of knowledge, and the testing of the amount and kind of knowledge possessed by a pupil, is relatively easy. Moreover, it is a process hallowed by tradition, for it has long been held by the bulk of the population that to be highly educated means to possess a great store of knowledge.

It is possible to sub-divide the general class 'knowledge' into categories:

(a) isolated simple facts of the type used in quiz games, e.g. the names of the capital cities of countries;

(b) knowledge of technical terms, e.g. contour, drumlin, entrepôt;

(c) knowledge of a series of connected facts, e.g. the characteristics of the monsoon forest;

(d) knowledge of techniques, or ways of organizing or studying phenomena, e.g. field-work techniques;

(e) knowledge of conventions, e.g. in regional description the 'logical' sequence;

(f) knowledge of trends and sequences, e.g. long-term climatic changes, the stages in the development of a depression;

(g) knowledge of classification and categories, e.g. the various systems of climatic classification;

(h) knowledge of criteria, e.g. how we decide whether a scientific theory has been proved;

(i) knowledge of principles and generalizations, e.g. winds are caused by variation in atmospheric pressure, the world wind system;

(j) knowledge of theories, e.g. the theory of continental drift and the evidence which supports it.

COMPREHENSION

The ability to understand a communication is of fundamental importance in a modern society. The communication may take many forms, e.g. a series of mathematical symbols, a diagram, map or picture, or a piece of writing. Examinations may seek to measure comprehension in three ways:

(a) by requiring a translation, e.g. from pictorial form into words, or from words into different words;

(b) by interpretation, which may require identification of major ideas in a passage for example, or a commentary on the meaning of a graph or symbolic communication;

(c) by extrapolation which requires not only the ability to translate and interpret, but also to foresee consequences of a trend or tendency, e.g. a graph of population expansion may indicate certain undesirable consequences of a continuous trend in one direction or other.

Similarly, comprehension of given data may enable a reasonable interpolation to be made in gaps in the data.

APPLICATION

This ability differs from comprehension in that it represents another step in the hierarchy of skills and abilities. It implies the ability of a pupil, not merely to understand, for example, a principle or theorem in mathematics, but also to have the ability to recognize whether or not the principle is applicable in any given case. In general it implies an ability on the part of a pupil to select the appropriate abstract tools in order to solve a problem, make a prediction or explain some phenomenon.

ANALYSIS

Analysis involves the ability to break down a given communication

into smaller, more comprehensible parts and to recognize t[ ]
relationship between the parts. It may be regarded as an aid [ ]
or demonstration of, more complete comprehension, and is ther[ ]
fore favoured both as a means of teaching and as a means [ ]
examining.

Analysis may be applied in practically any subject. Three ste[ ]
in a complete analysis may be formulated:

(a) breakdown into constituent elements to identify and classif[ ]
(b) demonstration of the relationships existing between t[ ]
elements identified;
(c) comprehension of the principles underlying the arrangeme[ ]
and structure of the whole.

The study of a region exemplifies the process.

SYNTHESIS

This is the opposite of analysis in that it may be defined as t[ ]
putting together of parts to form wholes. It is therefore close[ ]
related to analysis, but is more creative. Often the same elemen[ ]
or parts may be put together in a multitude of different ways, [ ]
that the synthesis may be a unique production. Almost a[ ]
creative activity involves an element of synthesis—the writing [ ]
a paragraph, a chapter, a book; the production of a drawing,
diagram, a picture or a model. It is probably the emphasis on th[ ]
educational process (as self-expression) which most distinguish[ ]
modern educational practice from that of the past. One reason f[ ]
this emphasis, of course, is that experience has shown that creativ[ ]
activity is probably the most absorbing and satisfying of all educ[ ]
tional processes. It is, moreover, one of the strongest argumen[ ]
for the 'essay-type' examination in that this involves to a hig[ ]
degree the ability to synthesize, to marshal and arrange materi[ ]
and to express thoughts in a lucid and pleasing style.

EVALUATION

By this term is meant the making of judgements, making com[ ]
parisons, using criteria previously determined or supplied. It m[ ]
be regarded as the most sophisticated of all the intellectual act[ ]
vities which it is possible to measure, and hence comes last in t[ ]
hierarchy. It may be said to involve all the other processes [ ]

class work has considered ports and their trade, the pupil should know the terms 'hinterland' and 'outport'. If he has studied Swiss valleys, he should know the meaning of the term 'alp'.

2. He may be required to learn and recall a selection of facts used and emphasized by the teacher. Does he know the location of principal North American cities, and can he place them on an outline map? If he has previously been exposed to ten selected facts of industry in the Netherlands, how well does he recall these facts?

3. He will have to learn the symbolism used in class lessons. What does he know of map conventions? For example, does he know that solid blue colour as used on a 1:63360 Ordnance Survey map may mean an entirely different thing to solid blue colour on an atlas map of mean annual rainfall? Does he know that topography may be shown on a map by the use of contours?

4. He should know something of the ways and means employed by geographers in dealing with the facts of their subjects.

   (a) Can he recall that an atlas is a reference book, and that by use of index, reference system and conventional signs he can find out information about places?

   (b) Does he know that climatic and economic information can be clarified and simplified by the construction of graphs; that contour maps may be made more understandable with the construction of profiles, selective tracings and sketch maps?

   (c) Does he know how a land-use map is constructed, using an outline map, a suitable classification of land-use, notation symbols and personal observation?

5. At a more advanced stage he should know of the classifications and categories regarded as important by geographers.

   (a) What does he know of territorial categorization (regional geography), to many people still the fundamental structure of the subject? Does he know that the world may be arranged into patterns—patterns of climatic types, of economic systems, of 'natural regions'?

   (b) Is he aware of the classification of landforms by origin— forms resulting from the glaciation of mountain country, forms produced by volcanic activity?

(c) Can he recall a hierarchy of settlements, ranging from dispersed houses to large cities?

COMPREHENSION

A pupil who knows geographical facts may show the state of his knowledge by the correct answering of questions which involve recall or recognition. He may, however, understand nothing of the meaning of his little pieces of information. He may be able to define a coral atoll as 'an island; being a nearly circular reef of coral; having occasional breaks or channels through which sea water can enter the central lagoon, and being found in seas warm enough to support the life of the coral polyp.' He may not be able to visualize the island, or even to put the definition into his own words. He should be able to do so. He may be able to recall that the mean annual rainfall of Edinburgh is 650 mm without being aware that such a figure is in itself a generalization. Geography teaching should try to produce such awareness.

The testing of comprehension involves testing three things:

1. An ability to *translate*. The pupil looks at a good coloured photograph of savana in East Africa. He may *see* acacia trees and bushes, elephant grass, the bed of a seasonal stream, baobab trees and the boma round the homestead of a local family. The teacher cannot know what the pupil sees until the pupil puts/translates the photograph into his own words.

2. An ability to *interpret*, to explain the relationship between the parts. He may see a relationship between the density and greenness of the grass and nearness to the waterhole (and water-table) and may then suggest a possible link. He may note the lack of arable land and the presence of cattle pens as evidence of a pastoral way of life.

3. An ability to *extrapolate*—to make a judgement. If the pupil were to see a number of pictures of savana in East Africa, he may be able to form an opinion of common elements in savana landscape.

Further Examples of Geographical Relationships requiring some Degree of Comprehension

1. Does the pupil understand the following relationships within

the domain of *physical* geography, and can he explain them?
(a) The effect of an ice mass moving over and round a plug
    of hard rock—differential erosion and the formation of a
    'crag and tail'

    (the hard igneous plug protects the rock lying on the lee
    side).
    Does he really understand the working of the erosive
    process in this context?
(b) The effects of regular, copious rain and great heat on
    vegetation cover and soil mantle.
(c) The effects of high latitudes on the light available for
    photosynthesis.
(d) The effect of an upwelling mass of cold sea water on the
    supply of plankton, and the consequent effects on higher
    forms of life.
2. How well does he understand Man's use of natural phenomena and resources?

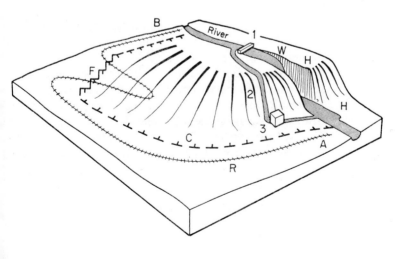

How are people *influenced by the places they live in*? Can he relate man to environment? (See diagram on page 21.)

(a) Why are estuaries significant factors in the development of many ports?

(b) Why does a liberal and varied supply of natural resources help to make a country rich?

(c) Here is a river falling over the edge of an escarpment. The waterfall is at (W). How will this physical situation affect Man?

    (i) If his interests are in *transportation*, getting goods from (A) to (B), he will try to avoid the waterfall; perhaps with a canal (C) and a flight of locks (F); perhaps with a portage or railway (R).

    (ii) If his interests lie in the field of *power exploitation*, he may put a diversion weir at (1), penstocks at (2), a hydro-electric station at (3) and use the force of the falling water to power his industries and light his homes.

    (iii) If he attempts to exploit the visual attraction of the waterfall he will need hotels (H).

    (iv) If the area shown here is very isolated and the people are not advanced in their technology, then the waterfall will remain an object of awe and nothing more.

3. How well does the pupil understand human and economic relationships?

(a) Has he some awareness of our reliance on other people and their reliance on us? Can he explain this interdependence?

(b) Why do the people of a region produce more of a foodstuff than they need for themselves, e.g. wheat in the Dakotas? Does the pupil understand how trade results from such surpluses being available?

(c) He may *know*, as a set of facts, that industry uses power, raw materials and labour. Does he *understand* that these factors must be present before industrialization can take place?

APPLICATION/TRANSFER

Good teaching should develop the pupil's abilities to *use* facts, skills and ideas. There is not much to be gained from the learning of specific facts and the comprehension of principles and abstractions unless these can also be used to solve problems in novel situations. Here are some examples:

1. The pupil may know what the National Grid System is meant to do. He may have been taught how to read a reference. Does he use this skill carefully and as often as needs demand it when looking at and reading an O.S. map sheet.

2. The atlas is a reference book. The pupil may have learned this, and may be well aware of the use of index, scale, key and latitude and longitude. How well, and how successfully, does he use this knowledge and these skills when asked to find information about a country of which he has no previous knowledge?

3. Suppose that a pupil has had some practice, in a rural setting, in completing a map of a farm with details of the crops being grown. If he is supplied with a simple classification and an outline map, can he survey the ground-floor building use in a city block? Better still, can he develop his own classification and select his own map?

4. A pupil may know how to go about the construction of a profile (cross-section) from contour information. He may even know how to work out the vertical exaggeration on such a profile. He may have used such profiles to help his understanding of the landforms shown on maps in the classroom. Does he apply this knowledge of a method, and an appreciation of its value, to a new situation, when he has to study an 'unknown' topographic sheet?

5. He may know how to go about the quantification of his surroundings, to measure slopes of hills and speeds of streams. He may know what a census is and how it can be taken. Can he take a census himself?

6. Can he construct a simple questionnaire and use that device in an interview with a farmer?

7. He may know what a field sketch is, and what it can be useful for. He may know how to go about making such a sketch. Can he, on a field trip, recognize places where such a diagrammatic analysis would be useful, and having seen the need, be able to draw and annotate his sketch?

8. Does he, at a more advanced stage, use classifications to bring a rather arbitrary order to his expositions?
   (a) In describing a town, does he systematically sub-divide it into its relatively homogenous zones; central business district, industrial area(s), suburbs, etc., and comment on each in turn?
   (b) On a field trip, does he in fact actively classify slopes as concave, convex and uniform; soils as clayey, loamy and sandy; topographical features as erosional or depositional?
   (c) Can he produce a systemic and thorough account of an area by considering in turn its position, geology, relief and soils, its climate and natural vegetation, its land-use and economy, its communications network, its settlement, population and social structure?
9. He may play a 'geographical game'—building a railroad across the USA. How well does he apply the ideas gained in this game to the study of railways in USSR?

ANALYSIS

This is a skill probably best thought of as an aid to comprehension. A pupil is presented with a communication. In geography this might be a textual description, a topographic map, a set of statistics, an aerial photograph, a model, or the actual landscape. He will analyse that communication by breaking it down into its constituent parts, by then attempting to detect the relationship between these parts, and by attempting to recognize the structure in which these parts are arranged.

Example 1
A pupil is required to read and study material on the production and sale of bananas. He is given descriptions of the growing and harvesting. He has details of the transportation systems, their ownership and organization. He has information about how the bananas are marketed and where they are marketed.

He studies this material and is guided to detect a time sequence; growing, harvesting, shipping, marketing and retail selling. He finds that this is very tightly controlled.

He also finds a geographical pattern. The location of areas of production in tropical and sub-tropical areas, with plentiful rain or irrigation water and with abundant supplies of skilled labour force. He is able to locate and map these. The loading and unloading ports are also found and the shipping lanes charted. The consuming areas are found and mapped. He finds evidence of the same commercial firms operating in the production areas, along the lines of communication and in the marketing systems.

Indeed he finds that each stage of production, transport and sale is controlled, for greater efficiency and a better product, by one set of owners (a corporation).

He has identified the existence of a monolithic closely integrated economic structure, developed to produce fast, efficient, profitable trading between complementary areas set far apart from one another.

Example 2
A pupil is given 'raw' material with which to study the Scottish Highland area. He studies the topography and identifies an alternation of deep glens and high ridges which also show many features attributable to highland glaciation. He finds flatter land to be concentrated at the lowest levels on the valley floors. He studies the settlement distribution and finds a repetitive and distinctly linear pattern. This pattern he compares with his first analysis and concludes that settlement is found only on the flatter valley floors. He continues to examine land-use and the lines of communication and finds similar concentrations. He may then attempt to visualize the typical landscape unit of the map area as having a narrow, fairly flat valley floor on which are concentrated the tangible and visible results of human occupation, while on either side rise steep uncultivated slopes. He may even attempt to express the result of his analysis in a 'model' profile, that is to *synthesize* from his conclusions, as in the following diagram (overleaf).

He has been able to develop a simple structure of physical and human relationships from his observations.

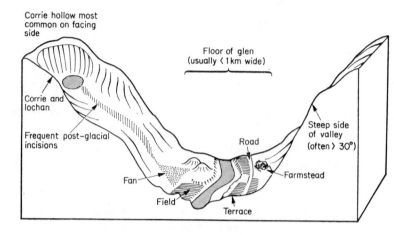

Corrie hollow most common on facing side

Floor of glen (usually < 1 km wide)

Corrie and lochan

Frequent post-glacial incisions

Steep side of valley (often > 30°)

Road

Farmstead

Fan

Field

Terrace

SYNTHESIS

This must be one of our more significant objectives. If a pupil can take the parts of a document—statistics, words, map forms, or the real landscape—and re-structure these parts into a pattern or form not obvious when he started he will be synthesizing. He will begin by examining facts, assessing ideas, indeed acting as a critical consumer. He will later function as a producer, creating something greater than the sum of the parts he started with.

Example
A student travels through a region on an observational trip. He keeps a route log of the things that he sees. These will appear in his notes as a chronological pattern. He will locate these things (phenomena) on his route map and thereby arrange them in a spatial order. Because his observations have been unspecific, that is not focused on only one aspect of the landscape, they will appear to be quite unstructured. The student may therefore attempt to produce by selection a structure not clearly seen in his original observations. He may attempt to correlate all his observations on the agriculture of the region and from these attempt to define its characteristics. Such a definition will be a synthesis of all his observations and thoughts on that particular topic. His definition will obviously contain some hypotheses and he may

then suggest that he test these by making a series of visits to randomly selected farms. After such a series of visits he will be in a much better position to produce a more revealing synthesis of the agriculture.

The activities associated with synthesis have great educational value.

1. They stress individual personal expression in contrast to passive absorption.
2. They stress self reliance in thought and action, in contrast to dependence on others for conclusions, decisions and actions.
3. They stress the pupil/student as a producer rather than a consumer.
4. They probably make learning more permanent, because they involve genuine problem solving. They probably make the pupil better able to apply problem solving processes to novel situations.
5. They provide strong motivation. Their challenge can absorb energy and create enthusiasm. Because they are creative they produce feelings of strong personal satisfaction.

POWER OF COMMUNICATION

Can the pupil acquire an ability to describe and explain the 'landscapes of varying geographical milleux, natural and human, on the earth's surface?' (UNESCO *Source Book of Geography Teaching*). We can and must test this outcome:

1. Can he write a clear, concise, well-ordered description of a geographical area, or physical, demographic, or economic phenomenon?
2. Can he reveal the interdependence between the facts of nature and the facts of human life—expounding and explaining any evident relationships?
3. Can he illustrate significant points with appropriate maps and diagrams?
4. Does he integrate such maps and diagrams fully into his total written work?
5. In presenting his work, does he observe certain conventions?
   (a) In making sketch maps, does he use neat clear print for labels; simple speedily drawn symbols and clear colour? Does he give full marginal information?

O.T.G.—2*

(b) Does he pay due attention to usages of grammar?
(c) Does he lay out his work well on paper? Does he use space in an aesthetically pleasing way?

EVALUATION

Objectives here are concerned with the pupil's ability to:
1. make judgements about the value of geographical material;
2. make judgements about methods used in the study and presentation of material;
3. use standards of appraisal and apply criteria (decided by the pupil or supplied to him).

For example, an able pupil has access to an economic geography reference book published in 1945. He should be able to discriminate between the misuse of that book as a source of contemporary description, and its use for comparative purposes in the determination of trends in economic development.

At a more advanced stage a geography student should be required to look critically at the topographical maps he uses. He should be able to select the scale of map most appropriate to his requirement: 1:250 000 for a general over-view of a region like S. Wales; 1:1250, for a detailed building-use survey of a city block. In making such selections he will have to apply certain criteria. For example:

1. A survey of individual buildings requires a map large enough in scale to show these buildings clearly and in stark outline. It should have no colour, because the pupil may wish to use a colour code for his recording.
2. General maps of a large region must be highly selective and show in a very generalized fashion the simpler patterns of relief, drainage, settlement and communications. They should not be cluttered with excessive detail. They may even be colourful and attractive.

CONCLUSION

At a very late stage in school geography the most able pupils should know much specific geographical information, possess a wide range of skills and the ability to apply these skills in novel situations. Able pupils should have the ability to analyse geographical materials and comprehend many geographical relationships. They should not only be aware of ways in which geographical data may be ordered, but should demonstrate some ability to use classifications, categories and patterns for themselves. They should have a demonstrable ability to write, and to draw maps. They may then be expected to synthesize facts and relationships to such a degree that they become able:

1. to observe and examine the landscape, activities and people of *any* place, record the results of their observations, give thought to the meaning of the things they have seen and then present descriptions and conclusions as clear orderly exposition in which text is well supported by well chosen and well made maps and diagrams;
2. to visualize accurately the nature of the world so as to enable them to think wisely about political and social conditions;
3. to recognize problems, propose theories, and test these;
4. to think in a constructive manner using geographical resources and techniques.

Such strength of command of the subject, its skills, facts and abstractions may well be possible for able advanced pupils. However, average pupils are unlikely to progress much beyond some knowledge of the subject specifics and simpler skills. They will know a variety of descriptive terms and a number of important geographical locations. They should certainly be able to use an atlas to locate places and areas. They should recognize many O.S. map symbols and be able to use a scale and compass. They may possess enough map reading ability to find their way across a piece of unknown land.

Average pupils may know many facts about distant places and be able to understand some simpler geographical relationships. Many of these facts and relationships will be deduced from the study of pictures. They should be able to draw simple sketch maps and write straightforward descriptions of the things they can see. These studies should bring some appreciation of ways in which people live and, hopefully, a greater understanding of their difficulties and the problems faced by the world community.

5. Characteristics of Objective Testing

To be useful, tests and examinations should fulfil two basic conditions: they should be both reliable and valid.

RELIABILITY

The reliability of a test is the consistency with which it can be marked, its comparability with other tests of the same series and the consistency of performance of the pupils taking the test, i.e. the test should produce results which correspond as closely as possible with the results of other tests or other means of evaluating performance which have similar objectives.

VALIDITY

The validity of a test is the accuracy with which the test measures what it is intended to measure. In other words, if a test is designed to discover the ability of a pupil to analyse maps, compare sets of statistics, interpret photographs or recall facts, then these abilities should in fact be tested. A good test is therefore constructed with this concept of validity in mind. Each part of the course, each objective, each desired outcome, will have its place in the test. Validity is difficult to measure and absolute validity impossible to achieve. The degree of validity obtained is normally dependent on the care with which the test is constructed. Validity is easier to achieve when more than one person is concerned in applying the procedures outlined elsewhere in this book.

THE ESSAY-TYPE EXAMINATION

The traditional essay-type examination is notoriously unreliable.

Research has shown that the same paper will be marked differently by different examiners, and that the same examiners will award different marks for the same work on different occasions. The reasons for this variation include the fact that some markers are more lenient than others, some markers look for different qualities in the scripts, and markers vary in mood from time to time. The mark awarded to a script will often be affected by the quality of a script which has just been marked.

The essay-type examination is also suspect with regard to validity in that it normally samples only a small part of the ground covered during a course. This factor also reduces the reliability in that chance plays a large part in determining whether a candidate performs well or badly, for he may be lucky or unlucky in the questions he chooses to attempt.

Other defects of the traditional essay examination include the fact that such elements as spelling, punctuation, and fluency of expression often influence the mark given. Some teachers would argue that this is an advantage in that every examination should be part of the educational process, and that these elements are important. The marking of essay examinations is a lengthy, laborious and boring procedure which nevertheless must be carried out by experts in the appropriate subjects, and is therefore expensive.

But essay examinations do have advantages. They are quick and relatively easy to construct and administer and they are familiar to all teachers and most pupils. It is claimed that they are good for measuring the more important mental abilities such as comprehension, application, analysis, synthesis and evaluation. Moreover they can be used for testing the ability to use knowledge rather than merely the ability to remember facts. The production of the written essay is claimed to be useful training in the use of English, in spelling, and punctuation. Whether this is a legitimate function of an examination in, say, history or chemistry is a moot point.

There is no doubt that the reliability and validity of essay examinations can be greatly improved when time and care is taken in the compilation of the examination, and where the marking is carefully controlled by experienced people, by the use of marking schemes and special marking procedures (e.g. marking question by question instead of script after script), and by the use of moderators, or second opinions, particularly for marginal papers.

OBJECTIVE TESTS

The objective test differs from the essay type in a number of ways. The number of questions (usually called 'items') is much larger—75 to 100 is quite common. This means that a very wide coverage of the subject matter is possible. Moreover, the relative importance of different parts of the course can be allowed for by increasing or decreasing the number of items for each part.

No choices are permitted. The pupil attempts as many questions as he can in the given time. The time allowed is so adjusted (after trials with other groups of pupils) that 90 per cent of the candidates can complete all the items. 'Spotting' of questions is therefore rather difficult and not very profitable in this kind of examination.

Each item has only one correct, usually short answer. This answer is predetermined by the compiler of the test. The important result follows that marking can be completely objective, speedy and accurate. By the use of templates, marking keys and so on, the scoring can be done by a few relatively unskilled, and therefore cheap, clerical workers. It is even possible to arrange for the marking to be done by machine.

Each item is allotted only one mark. It may seem illogical to award the same mark to an easy item as to a difficult one. However, because of the large number of items and the fact that candidates attempt all of them, it has been found that these tests do in fact spread the scores and a good distribution is obtained from normal groups of pupils.

There is no doubt that it is much easier to test factual knowledge by the objective type of test than to test the higher intellectual faculties, so that many published tests seem to give more weight to mere memory capability than to such factors as comprehension and application. For the same reason teacher-produced informal objective tests are even more likely to suffer from the same defect. Again, the tests do not enable the pupil to demonstrate his ability to write clear, well organized, grammatically sound prose, or to develop an argument. These are very important abilities which should be fostered by every means. On the other hand it could be argued that examinations can be provided to test these very facilities and therefore there is no need to make every examination also a test of English. Moreover, the use of essay-type examinations penalizes the poorer student of English in every subject.

Another criticism of the objective test is that it enables pupils to amass quite a considerable score by guessing. In the case of true/false items this could be 50 per cent; where four responses are provided the guessing score could be 25 per cent. For this reason many compilers of objective tests avoid the true/false type of item and always use five alternatives in multiple-choice items. However, experiment has shown that guessing does not, in fact, greatly influence the rank order of students, particularly if they are warned not to guess. One reason for this is probably the fact that an element of guessing enters into many answers, and it is impossible to draw a hard and fast line as there exists a whole spectrum between answers which are pure guesswork and answers that are the result of knowledge. It is, however, possible to compensate for guessing and a procedure is discussed in Chapter 9.

It has been said that objective-type tests have a very bad effect on teaching. The fact that the tests appear to demand the ability to memorize snippets of information, sentences from textbooks and so on, and do not appear to demand any of the so-called 'higher' abilities might tempt many teachers to change their methods of teaching to suit. Facts would be stressed, rote learning encouraged, writing ability would get little attention: this is known as the backwash effect. One answer to this kind of criticism might be to suggest that the objective test could be modified to include an essay element, or that the objective test should form only part of the final assessment of the pupil's work—the rest being made up of written exercises, projects, marks for oral work, teachers' assessments, etc.

Finally it is pointed out that the construction of a good objective test involves a great deal of painstaking effort, often by a whole group of experts. This is time-consuming and expensive.

The characteristics of the essay and objective type test are summarized in the table below.

Essay-type test	Objective-type test
1. Cheap and easy to construct	Difficult and expensive to construct
2. Tests ability to write clear, logical prose and to develop an argument	Does not test these abilities
3. No undue stress on memorization	Tendency to stress factual knowledge
4. Spelling, punctuation, grammar influence marking	These do not influence marking
5. Difficult and expensive to score	Cheap and easy to score
6. Marking not objective—unreliable	Marking objective—reliable
7. Slow marking at a time when speed is required	Fast marking when speed is required
8. Poor coverage of content	Good coverage of content
9. 'Spotting' is possible	'Spotting' difficult
10. No 'backwash' effect on teaching	'Backwash' effect on teaching

6. *Forms and Types of Objective Style Items*

There are two basic forms of item. First the recognition or selection in which the pupil chooses an answer from a selection placed before him. Secondly, the constructed response form in which the pupil is expected to recall or find an answer to a question and supply the answer in his own words.

The purpose of this chapter is to describe the characteristics of the main types of items within each of these two forms and to help develop some skill in item writing.

RECOGNITION OR SELECTION ITEMS

The three types in this group are truly objective in scoring. Pupils are asked to recognize truths or untruths within statements given to them, and to react accordingly. No interpretation of answers is required. These types are multiple choice questions, matching questions, and alternate response questions.

1. *Multiple Choice:*
This is probably the most popular kind of test item.
 Example 6.1
 There is only one correct answer to the following question. Choose the correct answer from the five given. These are lettered A, B, C, D, E. Mark the correct one by ringing the appropriate letter in the box below the question. (a)

 Libya is now a rich country mainly because of: (b)

  A its central position on the North African Coast;
  B the discovery of important oil fields;
  C the reclamation of agricultural land from the desert; (c)
  D its good transport system;
  E its trade across the Sahara Desert.

| A   B   C   D   E | (d) |

(a) is the guiding rule, or instruction to the pupil. In it he must be told the requirements of the question (or set of questions). This must be precisely worded. It may be referred to as the *rubric*.

(b) is the *stem*. It may be given as an incomplete statement as shown above. It may be a direct question. 'Why is Libya becoming a prosperous country? Select the correct reason.'

(c) is the set of optional answers. One is correct, in this case B. The others are plausibly incorrect, and are referred to as *distractors*. They are not intended to confuse or harass the pupil, but make selection of the correct response as difficult as may be required.

(d) is the place where the pupil records his *answers*; either by ringing the appropriate letter as shown above, or possibly by shading the letter space thus:

| A | B | C | D | E |

For a test these answering spaces may be gathered together on to one sheet for the convenience of the scorer. *Layout* of the item may follow the general pattern shown above. Each part should be clearly separated from the others. The format must be uncluttered: pupils should not be confused by being unable to distinguish the stem from the distractors.

COMPILATION

In compiling a multiple choice item the following procedure should be followed:

(a) Select a piece of specific information to be tested; for example a knowledge of the appearance of a cirque (corrie), and also an understanding of the symbolism of landscape drawing by which such a feature may be represented.

(b) Word a question clearly and precisely. Which of the following sketches shows a cirque?

(c) Write down (or in this case draw) the correct response.

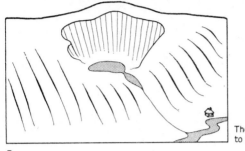

The building is to give scale

I.

(d) Attempt to anticipate responses which might be chosen by those pupils who may not recall the correct information.

(e) Make the wrong answers look plausible, not ridiculous.

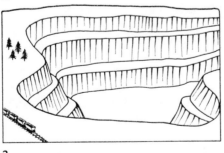

Helicopter to give scale

2.

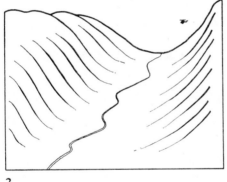

Train and trees give scale

3.

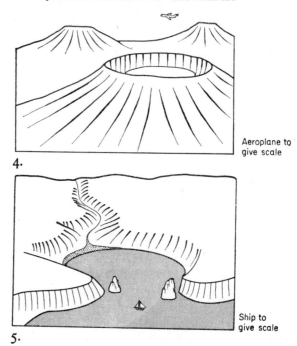

Aeroplane to give scale

4.

Ship to give scale

5.

The distractors are all pictures of landform features. They all show hollows. They could also be used as material for other questions. 'Which of the features is clearly man-made?' 'Select the landscape produced by recent volcanic action.' Omit No. 1 and 'Which of these features might be found in the English Lake District?'

(f) Have only one possible answer in your selection of responses.

Example 6.2
This item has two possible answers.

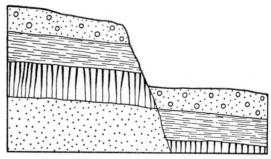

The geological section given above shows evidence of:
A movement of the earth's crust
B folding
C erosion
D vulcanism
E sedimentation.

A   B   C   D   E

Both A and E are possible answers. A fault is apparent and the symbolic shading in layers is that conventionally used for sedimentary rock.
(g) Avoid ridiculous responses. They waste time and effort and by cutting down the range of choice they make the question less effective.

Example 6.3
Cold air flowing down a mountainside, especially at night, can produce:
A heavy rainfall
B frosts
C depression conditions
D rising temperature
E a severe headache.
E is a useless distractor, being totally unrelated to the others.
It may be helpful to set the original question in a constructed response form; ask a group of pupils to answer it and use the resultant wrong answers as guides to the construction of one's own distractors.
(h) Avoid giving grammatical clues. The stem of the item must form a grammatical sentence with each of the alternative responses.

Example 6.4
The most populous country in Asia is the
A People's Republic of China
B India
C Japan
D Union of the Soviet Socialist Republics.
This is effectively a two-part (alternate response) item as B and C are eliminated by the grammatical construction.

Example 6.5 (an extreme case)
Valley glaciation has been a powerful force in
A producing the present landforms of the Alps
B because limestone dissolves easily
C make gorges
D scenery of Southern England.
No geographical knowledge is needed here. The grammar apparently rejects the three distractors.

(i) Item stems should if practicable be expressed in a positive form. Negative forms should be used as infrequently as possible. If they have to be used, the negatives should appear in italics, or capitals, or be underlined. The pupil must be left in no doubt.

Example 6.6
Which of the following features did *not* contribute to the rise of Greater Paris as the chief industrial region of France?
A Convergence of routes
B A navigable river
C A large labour force
D The underlying coalfield
E A large local market for consumer goods.

(j) Do not make one response stand out by being so much more precise than any others.

Example 6.7
In recent years there have been very great changes in the economy of North Italy. Select the statement that most fully expresses what has happened.
A Resources of hydro-electric power, natural gas, sufficient labour and access to world trade routes have helped to create manufacturing centres
B Mulberries and hemp support a textile industry
C Natural gas has been discovered recently
D FIAT is a most important car plant
E There has been a population movement from South Italy to the North Italian Plain.
The pupil can see that B, C, D and E each give one factor or fact and cannot therefore be distinguished from one another in terms of 'fullness' of expression. A is clearly so much more complete.

2. *Matching type:*

This is a special variety of the multiple choice type. Each item of this kind should be made up of three parts:

(a) the directions to the pupil,
(b) the list of stem items (numbered),
(c) the list of choices (lettered).

Example 6.8
Identify the agents of land formation specially responsible for each of the features in the *numbered* list. Write the appropriate *letters* in the correct spaces.

——— 1. erg

             A valley glacier

——— 2. canyon   B continental glacier

             C wind in arid conditions

——— 3. cirque   D wind in humid conditions

             E coastwise current

——— 4. horn peaks F vulcanism

             G humanity

——— 5. spit   H water erosion in an arid area

             I   water erosion in a humid area.

——— 6. caldera

Note:
(a) There should be one correct choice for each numbered stem.
(b) There should however be some plausibility in some of the other items.
(c) The lettered list may have choices which can be used more than once. For example, A can be used as the answer to both 3 and 4.
(d) The lettered list should contain some choices which are never used at all. It should never be possible for a pupil to answer the last stem by a simple process of elimination. In the above example B, D, G and I are not usable choices.
(e) Each set should be homogeneous. For example, some items on climatic cause and effect should not be combined with items on landform cause and effect.

Example 6.9 (showing lack of homogeneity)
Here are two lists, one of causes and one of effects. Identify

by use of the appropriate letter the most likely effect arising from each of the numbered causes.

Causes

——— 1. A weakness in the earth's crust ....
——— 2. Heavy rain on an unconsolidated surface............
——— 3. Seasonal alternation of high and low pressure systems over land ....
——— 4. The upwelling of a mass of cold sea water.........

Effects

A brings large quantities of nutrient salts within reach of the plankton
B produces rapid erosion
C produces land and sea breezes
D induces earth movements or vulcanism
E produces good crops
F makes for a dense population.

This is a particularly ineffectual question because E and F, the only unusable distractors, bear no possible relationship to any of the four stems, and two of the stems and the remaining effects may be easily paired off, viz.

4 with A (plankton live in the sea)
3 with C (the only climatic items).

(f) In geography tests there are several possible bases for this type of item; geographical terms and their definitions, countries and their populations, actual cities and the most relevant theories of growth, settlements and their sites, causes and effects, and so on.

3. *Alternate response type:*

This is sometimes called the 'true/false' type. It is a popular type for use in a classroom test, but it has a serious disadvantage in its 50 per cent chance (guessing) factor (see Chapter 9 for further discussion of this point).

Example 6.10

Place a tick (√) in the selected box thus: | √ |
Standards of living in rural India are higher than those in urban Canada.

true | | false | |

Example 6.11
Distance east or west of Greenwich is measured in degrees of
Longitude.

true/false.

Such statements must be very simply worded. They should not
contain a true section along with a false section. Test a single fact
or idea in a single clause. Do not put both reason and result into a
single question. Avoid conjunctions such as 'therefore' and
'because'.

Example 6.12 (showing this fault)
The wet season in Indian monsoon climate occurs in the
summer becuase the off-shore winds carry much water vapour.

Statements used in this type of item must be clearly true or
false to the more able pupil yet at the same time should be plausible
enough to make them more difficult for less able pupils.

CONSTRUCTED RESPONSE ITEMS

Constructed response items require pupils to make short statements about specific topics or to complete blanks left in statements
given by the examiner. They are rarely completely objective in
character. They require an examiner to make an interpretation of
an answer. The answer may be nearly correct, or may use an
acceptable synonym for the desired word or term. Nevertheless
the examiner must exercise some degree of judgement. If a tester
makes a completion item 'objective', he is also very likely to make
it highly restrictive in terms of possible responses.

1. *Completion type*
(a) In this, the question is stated as an incomplete sentence or
   paragraph from which certain phrases, words or statistics are
   omitted. The pupil is required to respond by completing the
   sentence or paragraph. Similarly an incomplete map may be
   presented and the pupil required to add detail to it.

Example 6.13
You are to add the following details to this contoured map.
(i) Draw the line of a stream running in one of the valleys
   shown. Use your blue pencil.

(ii) Print the letter S over one of the spurs shown.

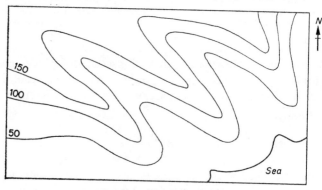

contours at 50 m. intervals

This cannot be truly objective in scoring as there are two possible locations for (i) and three for (ii).

(b) Several rules need to be observed in the construction of this type of item.

   (i) Pose the problem in the early part of the sentence and leave the blank till the end or near the end.

   NOT:

   In Florida .... is the name given to the type of farming which specializes in the growing of vegetables.

   RATHER:

   In Florida a type of farming which specializes in the growing of vegetables is called ....

  (ii) Ask only for key words or phrases. Too many blanks make for ambiguity and guessing. (The following example is an extreme case.)

   NOT:

   Igneous .... and .... are the result of ....

   RATHER:

   Igneous dykes and sills are the result of ....

  (iii) Avoid vague stems. If the stem is ill-defined, the blanks may be filled with vague answers.

   NOT:

   The climate found in Sicily is ....

   (... called Mediterranean ... is pleasant ... has hot summers ... is good for growing citrus fruits, are possible answers).

RATHER:

The name of the climate type found in Sicily is ....
(even this can be answered as ... Mediterranean or ...
Warm Temperate West Margin or ... Warm Temperate
Western Maritime).

(iv) Blanks should be standard in size for all items, whether the
word required is long or short or even if a phrase is
needed. This might be 20 or 40 spaces for a typed test or
perhaps six centimetres for a handwritten one.

i.e. ....

or ....

or ─────────────────────

It should certainly be long enough to take, with average
handwriting, the lengthiest answer required in that particular test. It should also be roomy enough to permit
deletion and second thoughts.

Blanks should certainly *not* be arranged thus:

The most populous continent is _____ .

With the exception of Antarctica the least populous
continent is _____ .

2. *Short answer type:*

(a) In this type of question the pupil is asked
Where .... ? What .... ? How much .... ?
When .... ? By whom .... ? etc.

(b) In order that precise answers may be given the questions must
be precisely stated. Study these questions:

(i)   What is the population of Scotland?

(ii) Where is Singapore?

(iii) Enumerate the factors contributing to the under-development of the Indian economy.

Pupils may ask. 'Do you want the population of Scotland to
the nearest million?' 'Do we give the latitude and longitude of
Singapore or will a general description do?' 'How many factors
are needed to give a complete answer to question (iii)?'

(c) These items are clearly unsatisfactory, and would certainly
have to be re-written, perhaps thus:

(i)   Give the population of Scotland to the nearest million.

(ii) Where is Singapore? Give your answer as latitude and
longitude and to the nearest degree.

(This should not be a recall item, but should test a pupil's ability to look up information in an atlas.)

   (iii) Enumerate five distinct factors, physical or social, that have contributed to the economic under-development of India.

(d) If answer spaces are to be left after the statement of each question, these answer spaces should be big enough to allow a pupil, having second thoughts, to delete an answer and write in an alternative.

It could be argued that these short answer questions are not objective enough and therefore should not be used in an objective test.

CONCLUSION

From this considerable variety of test items, the class teacher will select the type best suited to the material being tested and the particular requirements of the classroom situation. In constructing the specific items there are certain basic rules he should be guided by.

1. There should be clear instructions to the pupil, who should be left in no doubt as to what he is required to do.

2. The actual question (stem) and the responses used should be worded clearly and precisely. There should be no ambiguities.

3. Attention should be paid to the quality and consistency of grammar, so that pupils may neither be misled nor inadvertently helped to guess an answer.

4. The whole test should be presented in a neat, orderly fashion. Confused layout makes understanding more difficult and wastes the pupil's time.

7. *Item Analysis*

An objective test is made up of a number of separate questions called items and the number of items in a test is quite large—usually about 100—both because items are answered relatively quickly, and because a large number of items is essential for both reliability and validity. Each item has an essential role to play in providing the information required by the tester and therefore each item must be carefully examined from several points of view before it is finally accepted as suitable for inclusion in a test.

ITEM CATEGORIZATION

The test compiler must balance the test in regard to several criteria. For example, some items must test higher objectives than recall, and decisions must be taken as to how many items will test knowledge, how many will test comprehension, application and other categories. An item must be categorized in this sense both before and after it has been written. Often an item will test more than one of these categories. In that case, the item is given the highest category (see Chapter 10). It is essential that item writing and categorizing should be a joint effort on the part of two or more teachers. It is far more likely that defects in writing and categorization will be avoided when a group has taken part in the decision making.

ITEM DIFFICULTY

The test compiler must know how difficult each item in the test is likely to be. There is no way of finding this out other than by trying out the test on a group of students or pupils of similar ability, in the subject being tested, to the group for whom the test is intended. The number of pupils used in the pre-test need not be very large—not more than 300 is usually suggested, but a much smaller number may be used. Care should be taken that the pre-test group should be as representative as possible of the main

47

group, in such respects as distribution of ability and types of school attended. Once objective tests are in regular use in an institution the pre-testing of new items becomes easy. They are included in tests without the pupils being informed which items are merely being pre-tested. It is possible to pre-test using a small proportion of the main body of pupils providing that the pre-tests are on small, scattered groups of pupils, each group only testing a few items, say 20 to 30. The best method is probably to pre-test on a group of pupils who are following the same course (or a very similar one) in another area, and who will not form part of the main body.

After pre-testing, the results can be examined and the difficulty of each item worked out. The term *Facility Value* or *Facility Index* has been used to describe this, and may be defined as the relationship between the number of pupils who answer an item correctly and the number who attempt the item. The Facility Value (FV) may be expressed either as a decimal fraction or as a percentage. For example, if an item is tested on 90 pupils, and 45 of them answer it correctly:

$$FV = \frac{\text{No. answering correctly}}{\text{No. attempting the item}} = \frac{45}{90} = 0.5 = 50 \text{ per cent}$$

An item that turns out to be easy will have a high value, e.g. 0.9 or 90 per cent; a difficult item will have a low FV, e.g. 10 per cent or 0.1. The proportion of easy and difficult items included in a test will vary according to the intended function of the test. If a small group of scholarship applicants are being selected, then a high proportion of difficult items will be indicated; if a group for remedial treatment is being selected, then a high proportion of easy items will be included. It is obvious that items too difficult for any pupils to answer correctly and those so easy that all the pupils get them right are useless in that they do not separate the candidates. Where the desired distribution is the 'normal curve', then it has been suggested that the average FV should be 50 per cent, and all should lie between the extremes of about 15 and 85 per cent. Other experts claim that the best procedure is to aim at making all items as near FV 50 per cent as possible. When an item has been found to be too difficult or too easy as a result of a pre-test, it is often possible to modify it and re-test. Where an item turns out to have an FV of 0 per cent, it is often found that an error has been made in printing the key.

ITEM DISCRIMINATION

f the test as a whole performs well and provides the kind of distribution the tester requires, it may be assumed that pupils of high ability will have high scores and pupils of low ability will have low scores. The test as a whole may then be used as a criterion against which may be measured the discriminating power of each item used. An item which has a high *Discrimination Factor* (or *Discrimination Index*) is one which a high proportion of the able pupils answer correctly and a high proportion of the less able pupils answer incorrectly. If an item does not have this discriminating power to any great degree then it is not contributing much to the aim of producing a rank order. It should be noted that an assumption is made here that the test as a whole is measuring one factor, e.g. ability in geography. It may be that where a test contains clearly disparate sets of items, e.g. some on mapwork, some on recall of geographical facts, and some on photographic interpretation, it might be better to calculate the discrimination factor on each of the subsets.

There are several methods of calculating the DF of an item. A very quick and simple method for large numbers of cases is to use what is called a 'Chart for computing Tetrachoric r'.* The whole group is divided into two halves, upper and lower according to the total test scores, i.e. one group contains the upper half of the scores, the other group the lower. Next the percentage of students in each of these two groups who pass a particular item is obtained. Using these percentages, the DF (r) may be read off the chart.

In cases where the number of pupils for whom data is available is small, inspection of the percentages in each half passing any particular item will give some indication whether the item-test correlation is positive, about zero or negative. If more are correct in the top half than in the bottom half, the correlation is said to be positive. Where the percentages are about equal, the correlation is about zero, and the item is serving no useful purpose. If the percentage answering the item correctly is higher in the lower half than in the higher half, then the item is actually serving to decrease the validity of the test, and should of course be discarded.

*Single copies may be obtained from State of North Carolina Personnel Department, Raleigh, North Carolina, free of charge. Additional copies are obtainable at 1 dollar per dozen. See Dorothy A. Wood, *Test Construction* (Merrill, 1961).

Another method of calculating the DF makes use of the top 27 per cent of the pupils and the bottom 27 per cent of the pupils, as it has been found by research that 27 per cent appears to be the best compromise between making the extreme groups as large as possible and making them as different as possible. The DF is then worked out using the formula:

$$DF = \frac{(N_H - N_L)}{n}$$

where N_H is the number of correct responses in the top 27 per cent N_L is the number of correct responses in the bottom 27 per cent, n is the number of candidates constituting 27 per cent of the entry, i.e. the number in each group. If all the top 27 per cent give a correct answer to an item, and none of the bottom 27 per cent, the DF for the item is 1.0, i.e. the maximum possible. Where the DF is below 0.2, the item would be rejected.

Some of the possible reasons for a low DF may be:
1. incorrect key;
2. more than one response is correct;
3. ambiguity in the item;
4. the distractors may all be obviously incorrect, that is the item may be too easy;
5. the item may be too difficult;
6. the item may be a 'rogue', that is it is testing objectives different from those tested by other items in the test—for example, it may be the sole mathematical item.

By combining the FV and the DF in one table*, the acceptability of an item may be determined:

DF	FV Below 40%	FV 40%–60%	FV Above 60%
Above 0.40	difficult*	acceptable*	easy*
0.30–0.39	difficult	improvable	easy
0.20–0.29	difficult	marginal	easy
Below 0.20	rejected	rejected	rejected

The items which fall into the categories marked with an asterisk (*) would normally be acceptable items for the test.

The importance of careful choice of distractors in the case of

*(Reproduced, by permission, from *Objective Testing* by H. G. MacIntosh and R. B. Morrison, University of London Press, 1969).

multiple choice items has been stressed in Chapter 6. All the responses should be plausible and all should be carrying load. If, on analysis, some distractors are found to have little 'distraction value' (less than 5 per cent, say), then the distractor should be replaced.

When items have been pre-tested and the FV and DF calculated, the construction of the objective test may take place. This is discussed in the next chapter.

8. Compiling an Objective Test

There are two main stages in the construction of an objective examination. There is the *planning* stage, at which the teacher will decide on the objectives to be tested, and content and concepts to be included, the emphases to be made; also the size or length of the final test. The *building* of the test comes next. The items have to be ordered, an answer key constructed and the final typing and duplicating done.

PLANNING

1. *Make analyses of content and objectives to be tested*

What are the specific facts to be tested ? Which simple ideas should the pupil be able to explain ? Which complex relationships should he be able to explain ? What are the skills and ideas he should be able to apply ? Can he apply low-order skills like 'translation' and higher-order skills like 'analysis' ?

This material may be more easily assembled and reviewed if presented as a table. Table I (pages 53–4) represents part of a content analysis of the major topic 'Climate and Man'. It includes the more tangible objectives: knowledge of facts, understanding of simple concepts; understanding of major ideas and application of these. It has been developed to include such skills as oral communication, map making, cross-section drawing and measurement; but such skills will normally be common to all tables of content in geographical contexts.

In order to be really efficient, a test maker would need to have a collection of such summaries.

2. *Weighting and abilities to be tested in each topic*

(a) How much weight is to be given to each topic ? The test maker must judge the relative importance of each section/topic.

(b) *Which abilities are to be tested?*

There is nothing intrinsically wrong in a test which includes only 'knowledge' items. It may be very limited in its value, but it may be the only kind of learning the teacher wishes to test at the time.

These decisions can be summarized as in Table III (page 55).

TABLE I.—Part of a Table of Content

CLIMATE AND MAN

	Transhumance in Switzerland	Nomadism in North African Desert
Knowledge	e.g. facts of valley shape and slopes in Alps; facts of climate and seasonal variations; names of places and alpine valleys; definition of foehn; kinds of trees; symbols used on Swiss topographical maps	e.g. facts of the climate, amounts of rain and frequency of rain; vegetation types; animals; location of water-holes (oases); definitions
Comprehension of simpler concepts	e.g. snow cover makes pasture inaccessible; temporary houses are located where land is used in summer only; the use of a cross-section to show seasonal migration; snow on steep slopes is unstable	e.g. herbivores can eat dry vegetation; all animals need a regular supply of water; travelling people need to carry their homes
major ideas	e.g. climate can control men's movements;	e.g. land with poor water resources has

	Transhumance in Switzerland	Nomadism in North African Desert
Comprehension of major ideas (continued)	Man reacts to extreme seasonal variations in climate; people must use the resources available to them	few people; primitive people must respond to nature in order to survive
Skills to be applied	drawing of sketches from photographs; cross-section drawing from contours; climate graph construction; grammatical skills (oral and written)	drawing of sketches from photographs cross-section drawing from contours; climate graph construction; grammatical skills (oral and written)
Analysis	detection from given raw material of seasonal changes and vertical/altitudinal differences, and relationships of these to human activity	study of maps, statistics, pictures and 1973 reports of drought in West Africa, chosen to illustrate short-term and long-term movements
Synthesis	writing of a personalized essay and painting of picture(s) expressive of the landscape and its rhythm	group writing of a playlet about the problems of dry wells; also a small exhibition of charts, model, photos
Evaluation	self/group appraisal of paintings, written work and graph work	selection of materials for exhibition and group appraisal of final products

TABLE II.—Example of a Table of Specifications.
The example given here deals with five topics and more tangible
objectives. It is clearly strongly biased to the testing of knowledge.

	topic 1	topic 2	topic 3	topic 4	topic 5	Total
Knowledge	4	4	8	10	—	26
Understanding of minor ideas	3	3	3	3	—	12
Understanding of major ideas	—	3	3	1	—	7
Application	—	—	—	—	5*	5
	7	10	14	14	5	50

*It must be understood that topic 5 is being tested in a novel situation,
and although the five items being used are classified here under 'application' they naturally assume the 'knowledge' of the facts relevant to the
topic and understanding of the ideas.

BUILDING THE TEST

1. *The items are produced.* These may be available in the teacher's
file or 'bank' of items. They may have to be written for his present
purpose. A teacher will find it very helpful to draft several items
after each class or lesson unit, or indeed include such drafting in
his preparation for the lesson. If each item is written on a separate
card or sheet of paper the next stage will be made easier.

2. *A sequence is decided.* One of several alternatives may be
adopted.
   (a) the teacher may follow the order of topics given in his table
       of contents. For example, in a test on the British Isles the
       order might be:
       Section 1 (items 1 to 20)   Scotland
       Section 2 (items 21 to 40)   England and Wales
       Section 3 (items 41 to 50)   Ireland (N. and S.)
   (b) Items may be grouped the way in which they are grouped in

Chapter 10 of this book; items testing knowledge coming first, items testing understanding next, and so on.

(c) Items may be presented in a random fashion. The different kinds of learning are mixed; content is mixed. The disadvantage of this kind of approach is that pupils are not likely to be helped by the pot-pourri of items resulting from this random procedure.

(d) If the teacher is already aware of the relative difficulty (Facility value) of each item, he could attempt to arrange them in increasing order of difficulty.

With any of these alternative systems it is helpful to the candidate to start with a few relatively easy items.

3. *The correct optional answers of the multiple choice items must be placed in random order.* They should also be nearly equally distributed among the various options—A, B, C, D and E. There must never be a pattern of correct options, e.g.

Item 1	(A)	B	C	D
3	A	B	(C)	D
5	(A)	B	C	D

Item 2	A	(B)	C	D
4	A	B	C	(D)
6	A	(B)	C	D

4. *Answer sheets should be duplicated*

■ Test No.	Pupil's Name .... ■
Title	Date of Test......................
....	Correct ☐ Wrong ☐ Score ☐

Item						Item					
1	A	B	C	D	E	25	A	B	C	D	E
2	A	B	C	D	E	26	A	B	C	D	E
3	A	B	C	D	E	27	A	B	C	D	E
4	A	B	C	D	E	28	A	B	C	D	
5	A	B	C	D	E	29	A	B		D	E
		B	C	D	E	30	A	B		D	E
					E	31					E

■Are registration marks, used to ensure exact registration of master sheet with pupil's answer sheet.

A fifty-item test can be accommodated on one A4 size sheet. This standard answer sheet is most economical of paper and permits test papers to be used again. It also speeds up the scoring process.

5. *The answer key should be prepared.* If a scoring machine is to be used, a master card must be punched. A duplicated answer sheet may be used by the teacher as a scoring template thus.

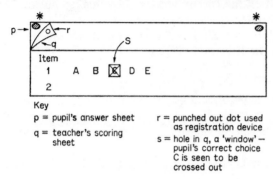

Key

p = pupil's answer sheet

q = teacher's scoring sheet

r = punched out dot used as registration device

s = hole in q, a 'window' — pupil's correct choice C is seen to be crossed out

NB. When marking is taking place with the use of a template, each answer sheet should be scanned to ensure that candidates have not just crossed all distractors.

6. *Directions to the pupils should be prepared.*
(a) General directions should be given. These should appear on the front of the test paper, for example:

INSTRUCTIONS TO CANDIDATES

1. Please read this very carefully.
2. You will need:
   (a) a question booklet (white paper)
   (b) Ordnance Survey Sheet IIIIA
   (c) an answer sheet (pink paper)
   (d) a ruler
   (e) a sheet of scrap paper for rough work (this should be on your desk)
   (f) a pencil
   (g) a clean eraser.
3. The questions:
   (a) All the questions are of the same kind.
   (b) There is only one correct answer to a question.
   (c) For each question choose the correct answer from the 5 choices given.

---

4. Your answers:
   (a) Complete the spaces at the top of the pink sheet, but leave the 'correct', 'wrong' and 'score' boxes empty.
   (b) Mark the correct answers like this ⊠ putting across through the letter chosen.
   (c) YOU MUST *NOT* USE YOUR ANSWER SHEET FOR ROUGH WORKING.

   (b) Specific directions should also be given as required for each item. The pupil should be left in no doubt as to what he should do.

7. The heading of the paper must be clear and complete, e.g.

   Geography Scotland..........subject/topic
   Class III B.....................pupil group
   27th June 1970.................date

8. *Typing* should be carefully done with great attention being paid to spacing and layout. Each item should be well laid out within itself. Different sections of the paper should be clearly separated from one another.

9. *Proof reading* is important and should not be omitted. Errors in spelling, typing and spacing should be corrected.

10. *Copying* should be by a clear process. Badly duplicated examination papers waste time and are a source of irritation to pupils and invigilators.

11. *Collation.* As a test is likely to consist of a whole series of sheets of items, these sheets should be carefully collated and firmly stapled together.

12. *Provision of other materials.* A geography test is likely to include photographic materials, topographic maps and sets of statistics. These items are unlikely to be on the same size of paper

as the question booklet and should be laid out separately on the pupils' desks.

The test is now ready to be taken.

There is a less onerous procedure for setting shorter classroom tests. Consider the position of a teacher who wishes to test a class on the work of two or three lessons. He may not wish to make out a detailed table of contents as in Table 1 and he may not be willing to work out a table of specifications as in Table 2. On the other hand he will have established his purpose for the test, namely to find out if all the facts, ideas and skills have been acquired by all the pupils, and if not, where the weaknesses lie. He should also have, in his own notebook, specific details of the objectives of his lessons. For example: In three lessons on volcanic activity and its effects on land forms he may have decided to introduce and teach:

(a) Knowledge of terms and facts:
    cone, vent, crater, intrusion,
    batholith, flow, aa, pahoehoe,
    viscous, fluid, basic, acid,
    tuff, volcanic bomb, conelet,
    active, dormant, extinct.
(b) Knowledge of locations:
    Currently volcanic—New Zealand, Iceland,
    Sicily, Japan, Mexico.
    Volcanic in past—Central Scotland, South Africa.
(c) Knowledge of appearance of volcanic forms with specific examples of each.
(d) Understanding of:
    (i) how fluid lava forms flows which have small angles of rest;
    (ii) how viscous lava forms flows which have high angles of rest;
    (iii) how instability/weakness in the earth's crust and sub-crustal currents produce flows of magma;
    (iv) how stability can return to a piece of the crust and volcanic activity cease.

As he will have used maps for (b) above he will have improved pupils' skills in that area. Photographs and diagrams will have been used to describe and explain (a), (c) and (d), and therefore pupil's abilities to translate from photographs to written language will

O.T.G.—3*

have been stimulated and may be tested. From this material, planned and taught, the teacher may select a number of facts and situations to test. He may produce test items as follows:

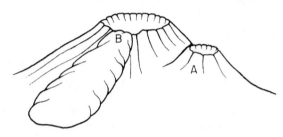

1. The feature shown as A is known as
   (a) a conelet
   (b) the slope of a crater
   (c) a secondary lava flow
   (d) a shield volcano
   (e) a plug.

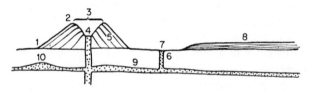

Match up the numbers on the diagram to the following list of features:

2. crater	I	2	3	4	5	6	7	8	9	10	11
3. vent	I	2	3	4	5	6	7	8	9	10	11
4. sill	I	2	3	4	5	6	7	8	9	10	11
5. dyke	I	2	3	4	5	6	7	8	9	10	11
6. intrusion.	I	2	3	4	5	6	7	8	9	10	11

7. The best reason why pahoehoe lava forms shield volcanoes is because
   (a) fluid lava flows fast over great distances before cooling
   (b) they are both found in Hawaii
   (c) it emerges at the sea floor, therefore cools slowly and is able to flow further
   (d) it is like treacle and spreads.

8. The volcanoes of the Edinburgh area are
   (a) dormant
   (b) sleeping
   (c) extinct
   (d) extant
   (e) active.

9. The presence of many volcanoes is associated with
   (a) numerous earthquakes and faults
   (b) dense human population
   (c) downwards moving currents in the lithosphere
   (d) numerous points of weakness in the rocks
   (e) the lithosphere.

10. In Central Scotland volcanic plugs are
   (a) the solidified masses of lava which once blocked the vents of volcanoes
   (b) the 'stoppers' that keep the magma from coming out today, producing new volcanoes,
   (c) formed when the rock moves and a mass of lava sticks up
   (d) most uncommon, as most of the volcanic activity was in sheet form
   (e) gentle sided hillocks smoothed and rounded by the action of water and ice.

This ten-item test may then be written out on spirit duplicator master sheets, checked and administered quickly at the end of the third lesson. Revision and consolidation and new explanatory materials may then be used at the beginning of the next period.

9. *Test Scoring and Test Analysis*

The marking of the style of test described in this book is by definition completely objective. When selection items are used, the marking key will be decided before the test is taken by the pupils. Marking procedures become decidedly routine; indeed marking machines may be used.

SCORING A CLASS TEST

In a class test, if the answer sheets suggested in Chapter 8, page 57, are used, then the scoring procedure is as follows. The scorer registers the scoring sheet with the answer sheet, puts a heavy red mark on all crosses seen through the little windows, counts correct items and enters the total in the space provided. He then lifts the scoring sheet, and counts and records the number of crosses *not* obliterated by the red marks.

SIMPLE ANALYSIS FOR DIAGNOSTIC PURPOSES

In a class test, the main purpose of which is to find out how well or how poorly pupils have learned, the following procedure will be helpful.

Using graph paper a matrix is constructed as below. On the X axis, the pupils are ranked according to their total scores; on the Y axis is recorded their performance on individual items.

This reveals:
(a) ineffectual teaching/learning in groups B and C;
(b) exceptions being item 7, and to a lesser extent items 4 and 6;
(c) 'patchiness' of group B;
(d) only top half dozen of the class did well;
(e) items 21 to 31 quite beyond group C.

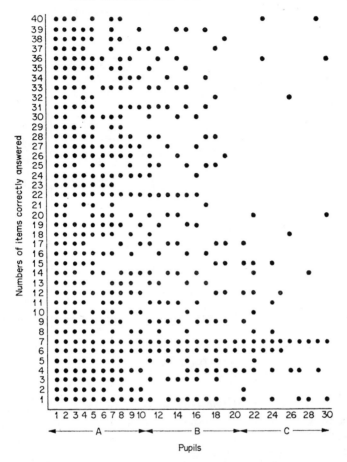

Pupils

From such a matrix it is possible to see, for example:
- (a) where an individual pupil's learning has been faulty;
- (b) where a less able group's understanding is incomplete;
- (c) where the entire class has misunderstood some aspect of the work;

OR (d) where the teaching has been inadequate.

ANOTHER PROCEDURE FOR RECORDING ANSWERS

This is more appropriate to end of term, end of session or to public examinations.

A test analysis sheet can be prepared as shown below.

Subject					Grade					
Date					Time Allowed					
No. of candidates										

Item no.	No. of pupils attempted	No. of pupils correct	FV	DF	A	B	C	D	E	Key
						Responses				
–	– – –	– – –	–	–	–	–	–	–	–	– – –

The exact format will depend on the circumstances of the test.

GUESSING AND
ADJUSTMENT FOR GUESSING

In a test made up of two-part alternate response items a pupil could, on average, by random guessing score 50 per cent. In a test of multiple choice items each having four parts he could score 25 per cent by random guessing.

The teacher may wish to recognize this possibility and use the following method to compensate for it.

1. If a pupil can score 50 per cent by random guessing, the scorer should regard 50 per cent as the smallest possible score and take account only of scores above that point.
2. Or the teacher may:
   (a) for a true/false test, total all the correct answers (X), total all the incorrect answers (Y) and apply the formula $X - Y = Z$ (where Z is the final recorded mark). This does not penalize the pupil who does not attempt items; who does not guess.

(b) for a test of three part items, apply the formula

$$X - \frac{Y}{2} = Z$$

(c) for a test made up of four part items, apply the formula

$$X - \frac{Y}{3} = Z$$

The general formula may be taken as

$$X - \frac{Y}{N - 1} = Z$$

where X, Y and Z are as stated above and N is the number of possible choices given in each item.

Although this procedure will give correct marks for the *average* pupil it will not of course compensate for luck.

It must be noted that this process is of no practical value* in the typical classroom situation in which pupils have sufficient time to read and respond to every item. It only becomes relevant where speed is a significant factor.

*See Dorothy A. Wood, *Test Construction* (Merrill, 1961), Chapter VI.

10. *Illustrative Test Items*

This chapter is simply a collection of objective test items to give helpful ideas to the teacher/tester. They have been roughly classified in terms of the main educational objective or objectives they appear to test. Within the chapter they have been arranged in five sections:

- A Items testing knowledge (knowledge of geographical quantities, criteria, facts, etc.)
  Questions 1 to 20.
- B Items testing comprehension
  Questions 21 to 37.
- C Items testing power of application
  Questions 38 to 57.
- D Items testing analytical abilities
  Questions 58 and 59.
- E Item testing student's ability to evaluate
  Question 60.

Certain sets of questions, such as those related to photograph study, contain a variety of items testing different objectives at different levels. These have been placed in the group to which they show the greatest affinity. Many individual items have multiple objectives. Each one of these items has been placed in a group, the main objective of which it tests most strongly. On occasion the 'most significant' process being tested has been selected in an arbitrary way.

No attempt has been made to provide any 'objective' items to test the ability to synthesize. This is without doubt best examined by a kind of test which demands actual creativity on the part of the pupil, for example:

1. a map of slopes to be drawn by the student after a personal survey of an area;
2. an essay to be written assessing relationships between steel production and port facilities;
3. a procedure to test the hypothesis that 'the quantity of material handled by a port is related to the productivity of its hinterland'.

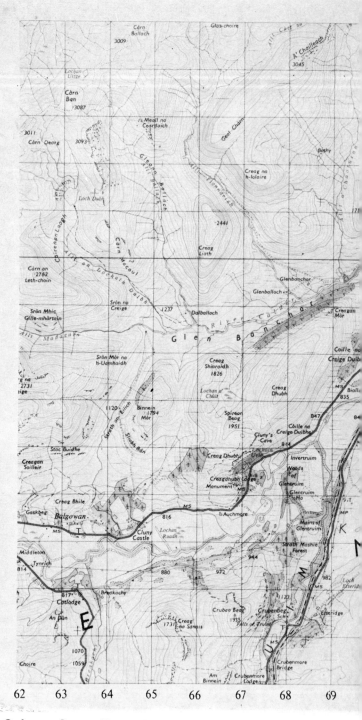

II Ordnance Survey Map 37A

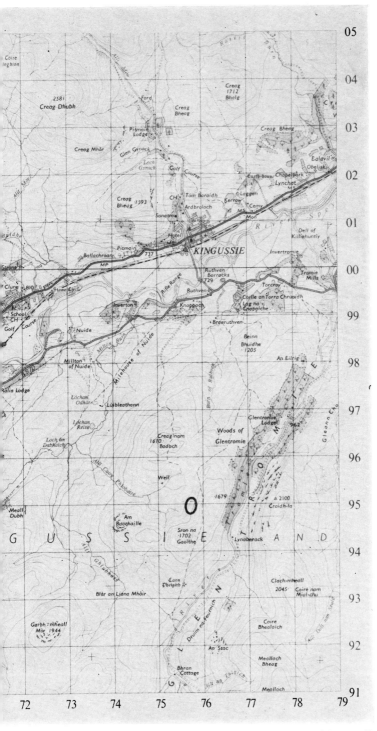

III Photograph (b)

Most of the items considered in this chapter test objectives of the greatest tangibility and lowest order in Bloom's taxonomy. These are the objectives the class teacher will most frequently wish to test with the vast majority of pupils, and by means of objective-style tests.

KNOWLEDGE OF FACTS

This group of items involves simple recall of location and nomen-clature. It is a type of map question very well known to all geography teachers.

Map of the Indian sub-continent (to be used with question 1)

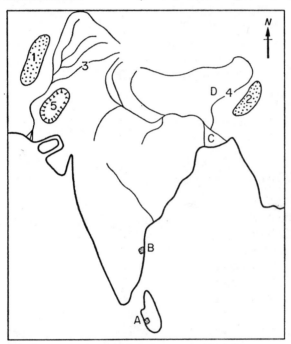

Question 1
(a) Name the hills dotted and numbered 1 ....
2 ....
(b) Name the rivers 3 .... 4 ....
(c) What physical feature is to be found at 5 ? ....
(d) Name the cities at A .... B ....

(e) Name one exported product obtained at each of the
    following places C . . . . D . . . .
(f) In which state is city A located ? . . . .

This is in constructed-response form and despite its having a
considerable degree of objectivity it could easily be restructured
thus:

(a) The hills dotted and numbered 1 are named the
    A   Suleiman Hills
    B   Aravalli Hills
    C   Deccan
    D   Himalayan foothills.
(a) The hills dotted and numbered 2 are named the
    A   Assam Hills
    B   Burmese Hills
    C   Cherrapunji Hills
    D   East Pakistan Hills.
(e) One exported product obtained at C is
    A   jute
    B   rice
    C   tea
    D   coffee.

Knowledge of Specific Facts

Question 2
About what proportion of the population of Scotland lives in
Edinburgh ?
A   10 per cent
B   20 per cent
C   30 per cent
D   40 per cent
E   2 per cent

As it is unlikely that a teacher will ask for such a *proportion* to be
committed to memory, question 2 demands recall of two population totals and an ability to work out a percentage. Question 3
demands simple recall.

Question 3
The Giant's Causeway in Northern Ireland is composed of
A   limestone

B basalt
C granite
D Old Red sandstone
E slate.

Knowledge of Geographical Quantities

(Also proficiency in judgement: what is the quantity relationship of each pair given ?)

Question 4
After the number on the answer sheet which corresponds to each of the following paired items, circle
  A if item in column 1 is greater than that in column 2
  B if item in column 2 is greater than that in column 1
  C if items are of essentially the same magnitude.

	Column 1	Column 2
No. 1	The thickness of the earth's crust under the Himalayas	The thickness of the earth's crust under the Philippine Trench
No. 2	The heavy rainfall of Manaos	The heavy rainfall of Cherrapunji
No. 3	The density of population in the Nile Delta	The density of population in the Mackenzie Delta
No. 4	The agricultural productivity of the Japanese farmer	The agricultural productivity of the Bengali farmer

Knowledge of Classification and Categories

Question 5
The branch of geography which deals with the formation of the land surface is best called
  A geomorphology
  B topology
  C meteorology

D   relief
E   formation study.

Question 6
The type of coal mining which involves the removal of a shallow overburden is called
A   open-cast mining
B   adit mining
C   shaft mining
D   placer mining
E   drilling.

Knowledge of Terminology

Also an ability to place industries in 'sets' according to certain known characteristics.

Question 7
Industries involved in the manufacture of cups, machine tools and television sets are known as
A   primary industries
B   secondary industries
C   tertiary industry
D   consumer industries
E   assembly industries.

Ability in judgement involving knowledge of terminology

Question 8
A volcano can best be described as
A   a crack in the earth's crust
B   a lava flow
C   a cone of lava and/or tuff
D   a burning mountain
E   being like Vesuvius

Knowledge of Conventions

Question 9
On 1:63360 O.S. maps a lighthouse is symbolized by

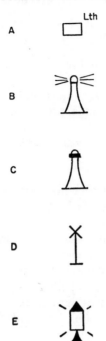

A

B

C

D

E

Knowledge of Criteria

Question 10
The map projections 'Mollweide', 'Bonne' and 'Sinusoidal'
all have the same merit because
    A   they are easily constructed
    B   they produce small distortions
    C   they give good visual effects
    D   they have straight loxodromes
    E   they are equal area projections.

Question 11
Assume you are a cartographer who is about to make a map
of the Congo Basin. Which of the following projections would
you consider most desirable?
    A   cylindrical.
    B   zenithal.
    C   conic.
    D   polyconic.

Knowledge of Methodology

Question 12
If we wish to find out how much traffic passes our school we would have to
A   ask the police for information
B   guess or make an approximation
C   keep a census
D   go to the local transport officer and see if he knows.

Question 13
If we wish to discover new facts about our home area (say within 2 miles of our home), our most scientific course of action would be to
A   read a good up-to-date class textbook on the geography of the country as a whole
B   go out, walk about and make careful observations
C   ask our teacher to tell us
D   talk about it with our friends in class
E   read the latest published guide books.

Knowledge of Generalizations, Facts and Terms

Question 14

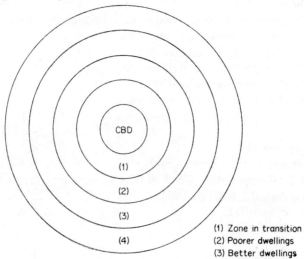

(1) Zone in transition
(2) Poorer dwellings
(3) Better dwellings
(4) Commuter zone

The above model is based on the work of
A Burgess
B Hoyt
C John Stuart Mill
D Haggett.

It represents the

A concentric	theory of city development	
B sector	,, ,, ,,	
C multiple nuclei	,, ,, ,,	
D globular structure	,, ,, ,,	

It is most usefully applied in study of the growth of
A Central North American cities
B the industrial cities of Western Europe
C Indian cities
D cities in the developing (third) world.

Knowledge of Trends and Sequences and Knowledge of Terminology

Question 15
During the post 1945 industrial developments in Scotland which of the following trends has *not* been apparent?
A Electronics industries have been developed.
B Heavy industries of the Mid-Lowland have declined.
C The coal-mining industry has become concentrated into a few large pits in Central Scotland.
D The textile industries of the Central Lowlands have continued to grow.

Question 16
Which alternative correctly completes the statement?
During the process of erosion and denudation of a landmass
A weathering and decomposition invariably precede all other parts of the process
B valley depths invariably increase until the land has been eroded entirely
C invariably landscapes of youth are succeeded by landscapes of maturity and later by landscapes of old age

D   the land surface emerges from the sea as a plateau and
        returns to the sea as a plateau.

The following set of histograms, each showing a different rainfall regime, are to be used with questions 17, 18 and 19.

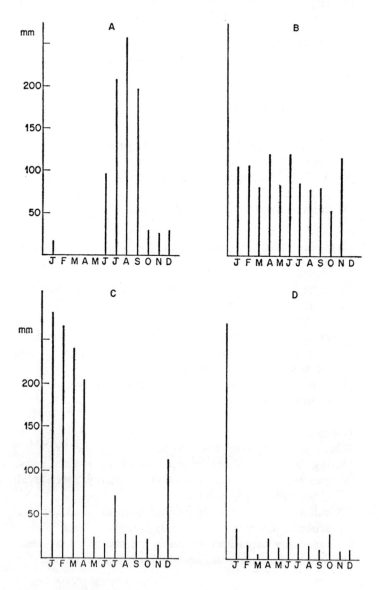

Knowledge of trends and sequences

Question 17
Which of the histograms of rainfall represents conditions found in Northern Hemisphere tropical monsoon areas?

Comprehension—Interpretation of sequences, involving judgement as to how close an example comes to 'ideal' characteristics in the pupil's mind.

Question 18
Which histogram best represents a climatic type with a well-distributed rainfall adequate for cultivation under N. West European conditions?

Comprehension—extrapolation of given data to another situation, depends on recognition of and admission of a significant relationship.

Question 19
Under which rainfall regime shown should river flows vary greatly from season to season?
1. A and B
2. B and C
3. A and C
4. A and D

Various Objectives

Application of skill in measurement, direction finding and use of reference system; also some knowledge of map symbols.

Question 20
Each part of this question may be answered using the map below.
All answers should be written in the appropriate blank spaces.

(a) The area shown on this map measures _____km
(b) The distance, in a straight line, between the railway station and the church, to the nearest whole number, is _____km.

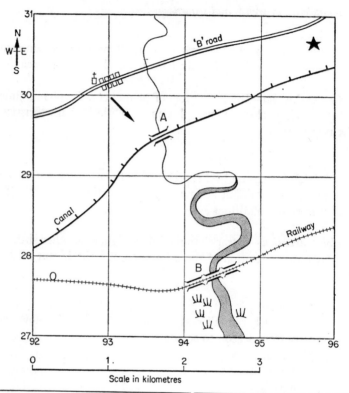

Scale in kilometres

FINDING A GRID REFERENCE	–	Example Point★	
EAST Take west edge of square in which point lies and read the figures printed opposite this line on the south margin Estimate tenths east	95 7	NORTH Do the same as for east, reading northwards along the west margin tenths	30 7
	957		307

Reference of point ★ is 957307

(c) If you stand in the village and look in the direction shown by the thick arrow, in which compass direction would you be looking? _____km.

(d) The road crosses the river by using a _____

(e) What is special about the appearance of
the Church ? _____

_____

(f) To which of the two bridge crossings A or
B would you apply the term 'viaduct' ? _____

Though these questions are of a constructed form they have a
considerable degree of objectivity, and a marking key is not difficult
to construct.

(a) This should be 16 km², but a lenient tester could allow 15.00
to 16.99 for ½ marks.
(b) This can only be 4 km.
(c) 'S.E.' should be given a whole mark. 'Between E and S' may
be given ½ mark.
(d) 'Ford' is the only fully correct answer, though 'not by a
bridge' may be given some credit.
(e) 'It has a *tower*' is correct. Mention of 'tower' should score
full marks.
(f) 'B' is the correct response, the crossing at 'A' is an aqueduct.

COMPREHENSION

Translation from diagrammatic form (cross-section) to verbal form
Involves also interpretation of data and making a judgement based
on this interpretation.

Here is a profile (cross-section) across a piece of landscape in
S.E. England.

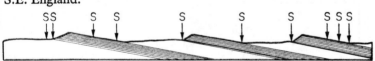

Clays
Limestone
S   Settlement

Question 21
Which of the following conclusions is *not* justifiable from the
information given on the profile ?

A   Settlements most frequently occur in low areas.
B   Porous rocks correspond to the higher land.
C   This structure is of alternating porous and non-porous
strata.

D　Many of the settlements in S.E. England occur where rivers have eroded gaps in the limestone uplands.

E　The prevailing geological dip is from west to east.

The 'translation' of an abstraction by giving an illustration or sample.

The example given here also clearly involves the application of map reading abilities.

Question 22

'In a lowland, limited sources of water favour nucleation of settlement.' Select from the maps below the sample which *best illustrates this generalization.*

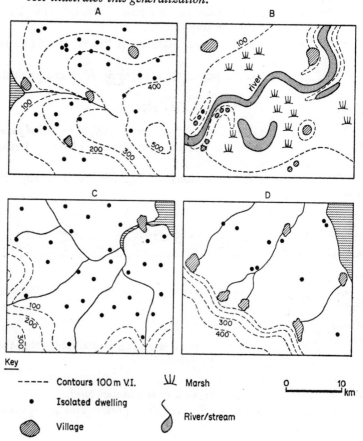

Recognition of pictorial symbols and extrapolation from this crude visual assemblage

Also involves knowledge of appearance of landscapes.
This pictorial diagram is to be used with questions *23* and *24*.

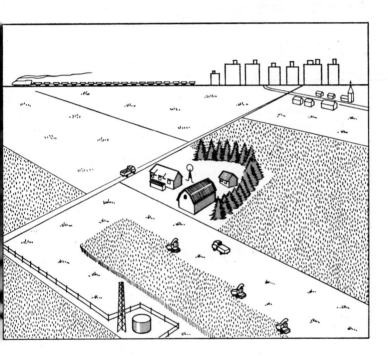

Comment: Any use of material like this is bound to involve the pupil first of all in a 'low order' form of analysis, in which individual features will have to be recognized for what they are or what they appear to be.

Question 23
Of which of the areas given is this picture representative?
A   The Dutch polderland.
B   The North American Prairie.

C   East Anglia.
D   The Murray Basin of Australia.

Illustration by use of an example

Testing of ability to translate from diagrammatic raw material, also ability to interpret this material.

Question 24
Which generalization is *not* illustrated by the example shown in the diagram?
A   Manufacturing industry is of growing importance in the American Mid-West.
B   Extensive cereal farming requires a high degree of mechanization.
C   Level land facilitates regularity of layout.
D   Produce collection points are normally at junctions in the transportation system.

Interpretation

Examine these maps of textile industrial areas in the USA and Europe.

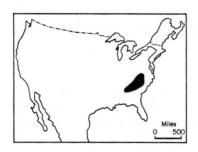 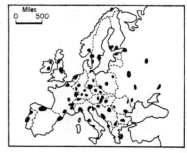

Question 25
Which of the following groups of factors is most clearly seen to have operated to produce these patterns?

A The comparative effects of political unity and political fragmentation.
B The limited availability of thermal or hydro power.
C The concentration of intensive activity in or near areas of dense population.
D Governmental influence in the development of numerous backward areas.

Translation by finding an example to illustrate a generalization

Question 26

In Southern Scotland Old Red Sandstones and their associated lavas tend to be more resistant to erosion than the carboniferous series. Which of these groups of features illustrates this generalization ?
A The Pentlands and the Esk Basin.
B The Tweed Basin and the Cheviots.
C Tents Muir and the Howe of Fife.
D The Cairngorms and Buchan.
E The Lead Hills and Clydesdale.

Translation from one level of abstraction to another

Question 27

A group of geography students are involved in a Land Utilization survey of a small rural parish. In ordinary English what are they doing ?
A Finding out how each separate piece of land is used and especially which crops are grown and where.
B Finding out how farmers do their agricultural work through the year.
C Making a head count of animals and estimating acreages of crops.
D Collecting soil and crop samples.

Interpretation of relative importance of ideas

Each question is followed by several statements. First, decide which statement is the general statement. Secondly, decide which statement does not explain the general statement.

Question 28
Why do people in climatically extreme parts of the world wear such different clothes ?
A   In hot, damp climates people need few clothes.
B   In cold climates good insulation is needed.
C   Climate strongly influences the kinds of clothes worn.
D   The clothes people wear are almost as important as their food and homes.

General statement A B C D

Non-explanatory statement A B C D

Question 29
Why are some countries rich and some countries poor ?
A   Ratios of production to consumption vary throughout the world.
B   In agrarian countries like India agriculture is not efficiently organized and she needs to import food.
C   The USA produces a great surplus of agricultural and industrial goods.
D   The work people do in countries like our own gives them a great deal of satisfaction.

General statement A B C D

Non-explanatory statement A B C D

Interpolation on a map

Question 30
Of the four maps shown below which shows the interpolated isarithm value 20 most precisely ?

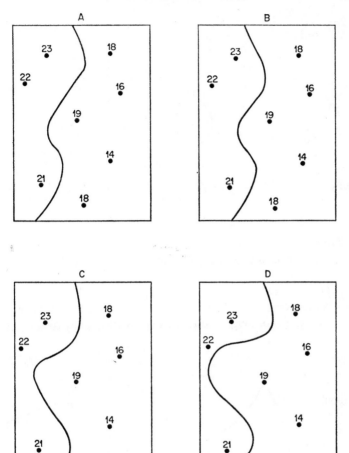

Comment. In this test, there are four points at which the position of the isarithm may be fairly precisely located. At tick W, on the map below, assuming a regular trend from 18 to 23 the position of W will be 2/5 along a line from 18 to 23. Similarly positions may be calculated for X, Y and Z. In consequence the distractors B, C and D are each made to show a wrong position for one of the above points.

O.T.G.—4

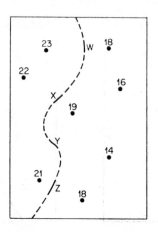

Translation from one symbolic form to another symbolic form
With reference to O.S. 1:63360 sheet 37A (Plate II).

Question 31
Which cross-section shows the shape of the land between 763952 (Spot height 1679) through Croidhla to 790950?

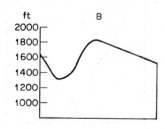

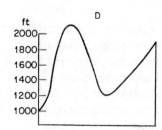

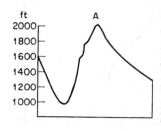

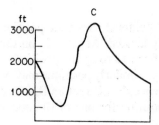

Comprehension, involving also knowledge of relative densities and movement of liquids and gases through porous rock, also of the conventions of cross-section drawing

Here is a cross-section of an oil field—a, b and c represent three substances found in the dome of porous rock.

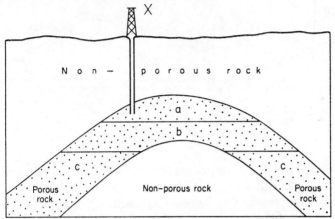

Question 32

Which substance will be brought first to the surface at the well-head marked X on the diagram?

A   Oil.

B   Gas.

C   Water.

D   Salt.

E   Sulphur.

Alternative Question

A drill operated from the derrick shown as X will tap the substances in which order?

A   Gas—oil—water.

B   Oil—gas—water.

C   Water—gas—oil.

D   Water—oil—gas.

Comprehension of some economic relationships and application of these to a given situation

This diagram is to be used with questions 33 and 34.

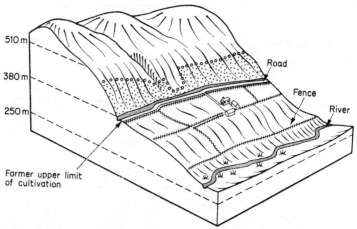

Whatever the main objectives of any item based on this diagram, such an item will also have to assume ability to read and comprehend the representational symbolism used, e.g. the pictorial representation of the farmstead, and the conventional use of slope lines.

Question 33
Use the diagram of a farm in N.W. Europe. The farmer has recently ploughed the land dotted thus ::::::::::::::::: Which of the following economic factors or situations is least likely to be helpful in explaining his action?

A A war has forced a reduction in food imports.
B An engineer has developed a powerful tractor capable of ploughing steep land.
C The government has increased subsidies to farmers of marginal land.
D New varieties of faster growing, more prolific grasses have been developed at a research institute.
E The farmer has recently acquired a large amount of private capital.

Comprehension and application
Extrapolation from a given situation

Question 34
A farmer in a wet area of N.W. Europe, cultivating the farm

shown in the diagram, ploughs the piece of land dotted thus
:::::::::::::::::::::: This is at a higher altitude than the former
upper limit of cultivation. The slope is too steep to contour
plough. Which of these are likely to be the *most immediate*
effects of his action ? Select *two* effects.

A   The exposed soil will absorb the heavy rains and run-off
    will decrease.
B   There will be increased expenditure on lime.
C   His farm will be able to carry an increase in stock.
D   There will be erosion and deposition of soil on the road.
E   He will require to make large purchases of fodder to feed
    his stock till the next season.
F   There will be an increase in the amount of marsh land
    beside the river.
G   The new pastures will be invaded by deer from the
    nearby hills.

*The relationship of farming to land, including translation of
visual form to number, interpretation, and assessment of reasons*

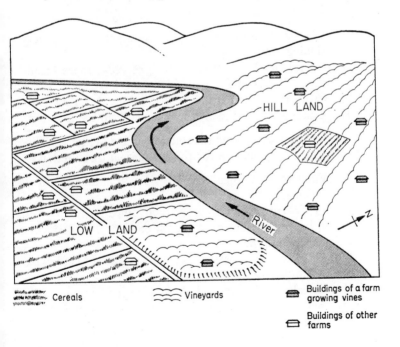

The above picture shows some farmland near the Mediterranean Sea. Some farms are on the hill land on the right bank of a river. Some farms are on lowland on the other bank.

Question 35
(a) Answer the following questions by filling in the totals in the table given below.

1. How many hill farms grow vines?
2. How many lowland farms grow vines?
3. How many hill farms grow cereals?
4. How many lowland farms grow cereals?

	hill land	lowland
vines		
cereals		

(b) Which of the following statements are *not* justifiable from the numerical distribution?

A   Vineyards appear to be more common on more steeply sloping land.
B   On hill lands vineyards are eight times more frequent than other farms.
C   Crops other than vines are mainly found on low land.
D   The lowland has many more farms than the hill land.

(c) Can you select from the statements below the *ONE* best general explanation for this numerical distribution?

A   Vines require considerable insolation and excellent root drainage.
B   The vineyard owners move their grape harvest downhill in baskets carried by donkeys, therefore steep slopes do not trouble them.
C   This situation represents a traditional use of land in parts of Southern Europe.
D   Cereals require fast and cheap transportation to markets, therefore they have to be on the main (lowland) motor roads.

Two examples of the use of photographs in objective testing:

Objectives mainly translation, interpretation and knowledge.
Study photograph (a), Plate I.

Question 36
1. This photograph was taken in
A   Belgium
B   Norway
C   Switzerland
D   Scotland
E   Greece.

2. The natural vegetation of this area may best be described
as
A   mixed temperate forest
B   grassland
C   coniferous forest
D   maquis
E   tundra

3. The main crop of the area shown is
A   cereals
B   root crops
C   grass/hay
D   small fruit
E   vegetables.

4. The houses are built of wood because
A   there is a shortage of stone
B   timber is abundant
C   there is danger from earthquakes
D   the winters are cold
E   wooden houses resist avalanches.

5. The houses have wide overhanging roofs because
A   the overhang keeps the house warmer
B   the overhang gives shade from summer sun
C   the overhang gives some protection from winter snow
and summer rain
D   the overhang gives protection from strong winds
E   the overhang protects from avalanches.

6. The photograph was taken in
A   spring
B   summer
C   winter
D   during the rainy season.

7. The building on the steep slope is used for
A   keeping cattle
B   storing vegetables and fruit
C   storing hay
D   as a workshop
E   as a tourist cabin.

8. There is no forest on the upper slopes because
A   avalanches have swept them away
B   the soil is too thin and the climate too severe
C   they have been cleared by timber men
D   they have been cleared for pasture.

9. The chief product of the farmers here is milk, but no cows
   are visible
A   they are in the milking byre
B   they are on high pastures at this season
C   they are lying down among the trees
D   they are never allowed out of the byres.

10. This area may be described as
A   hilly
B   mountainous
C   rolling
D   plateau
E   high plains.

11. The relief of this area has been chiefly shaped by
A   ice
B   wind
C   ice and water
D   water
E   earthquakes
F   volcanoes

12. The chief occupations in this area are likely to be farming
    and
A   forestry and tourism

B   hunting and village industries
C   mining and fishing
D   market gardening and weaving
E   hunting and weaving.

Simpler question for lower classes

Study the photograph (a), and the sketch (a1).
1. Making use of words from this list, complete the key to
   the diagram:
   pasture, clearing, electricity pylon, haybarn, cliff, peak,
   deciduous trees.
   Key
   (a) .... (b) ....
   (c) .... (d) ....
   (e) .... (f) ....
   (g) ....
2. Alternative way of setting.
   Write the number of each of the following features in the
   correct place on the sketch.
      1. pasture 2. clearing 3. electricity pylon 4. haybarn
      5. cliff 6. peak 7. deciduous trees.
The first question would be used where it was desired to preserve
the sketch (e.g. where it was part of a test paper to be used again
later).

Question 37
After studying photograph (b), Plate III.
1. This photograph was taken in the United States. It was
   taken in the state of
A   New York
B   Illinois
C   Arizona
D   North Dakota
E   Florida.

2. The natural vegetation of this area would be described as
A   steppe
B   chaparral
C   semi-desert
D   maquis.

3. The climate of this area is hot and dry. Which of the following features is *not* evidence of this?
A   Cactus plants in garden at left of road.
B   Wide verandahs and porches.
C   Small windows.
D   Scanty vegetation.
E   Sloping roofs.

APPLICATION

Application of knowledge of a method of grid location

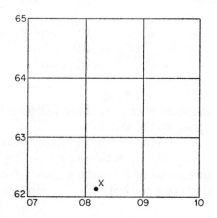

Question 38
Assuming that this grid is intended to be used in the same way as the National Grid System, the six figure reference for the point at X will be
A   082622
B   622082
C   083623
D   623083
E   098368
F   638098

Extrapolation of possible economic activity from a physical situation.

The actual situation presented is synthetic and therefore novel.

This also involves an understanding of the conventions of block diagram construction, including the representation of geology on the sides of the block. The diagram is to be used with questions 39 and 40.

Block diagram of a newly discovered oil field
(Scale along front of block)

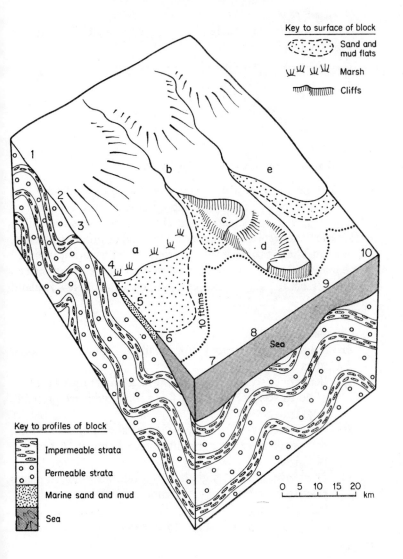

Question 39
Wells are most likely to be productive if drilled at
A   1 3 6 8 9
B   2 5 7 10
C   1 2 3 4
D   5 6 7 8 9 10

Question 40
Which area is most likely to be selected as a site for port and
refinery installations ?
A   Location a on block diagram
B   „   b „   „   „
C   „   c „   „   „
D   „   d „   „   „
E   „   e „   „   „

Application of various map reading skills

These include the use of map conventions, reading of keys and
abstract shadings. A number of these items require a degree of
judgement, but the most significant ability required is the ability
to translate from a cartographic form to verbal or numerical forms.

These questions can be answered from the information supplied
on the maps of New Zealand. The answers to all the questions can
be derived from the maps. No previous knowledge of New Zealand
is required.

Question 41
It would be true to describe the small area shown ⊗ in North
Island as
A   being over 5000 ft. high, having an annual rainfall average
    of 60 to 100 in., with very few people, who are probably
    not farmers
B   being over 3000 ft. high, having a rainfall of over 60 in.,
    having little or no agriculture and being very sparsely
    populated
C   being over 3000 ft. high, having a rainfall which in places
    rises to over 100 in. per annum, and densely populated
D   being over 3000 ft. high, having a rainfall around 50 in.,
    being uncultivated with very few people.

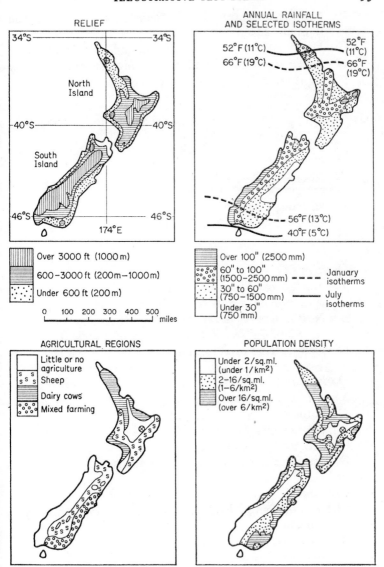

RELIEF

ANNUAL RAINFALL
AND SELECTED ISOTHERMS

North Island

South Island

174°E

Over 3000 ft (1000 m)

600–3000 ft (200m–1000m)

Under 600 ft (200m)

0   100 200 300 400 500 miles

Over 100" (2500 mm)

60" to 100" (1500–2500 mm)   --- January isotherms

30" to 60" (750–1500 mm)   ——— July isotherms

Under 30" (750 mm)

AGRICULTURAL REGIONS

Little or no agriculture

Sheep

Dairy cows

Mixed farming

POPULATION DENSITY

Under 2/sq.ml. (under 1/km²)

2–16/sq.ml. (1–6/km²)

Over 16/sq.ml. (over 6/km²)

Question 42
After studying the maps of relief and agricultural regions
select the most accurate statement.
A   Sheep are reared throughout the country.

B　More sheep-rearing land is found in North Island than in South Island.

C　Dairy cattle are reared on the lowlands of North Island.

D　Sheep farms are found on the highest lands of New Zealand.

(Use *both* of the top maps to obtain the answer to Question 42.)

Question 43
The steepest coastlines occur in
A　the east of North Island
B　all round South Island
C　the south-west of South Island
D　the north.

Question 44
The top left-hand map shows us that
A　land in these islands is very poor
B　New Zealand is in the Pacific
C　some land in New Zealand rises to over 3000 ft.
D　New Zealand produces butter.

Question 45
South Island is situated
A　in the Southern hemisphere
B　between 174°W and 172°W
C　between 34°S and 42°S
D　between the mountains and the plains.

Question 46
The area of South Island in square miles is approximately
A　10 000
B　20 000
C　60 000
D　100 000

Question 47
The rainfall of South Island can be best described as
A　heavy

B   heaviest in the middle
C   moderate
D   heaviest on the west side of the highland.

Question 48
The areas of little or no agriculture are also areas of
A   dense population
B   low rainfall
C   high rainfall
D   flat land.

Question 49
The mean temperatures of New Zealand's summer
A   are shown by the solid line isotherms
B   vary from higher than 66°F (19°C) in the north to lower than 56°F (13°C) in the south
C   decrease towards the North Pole
D   show that it is very hot there.

Question 50
The areas where most people live are
A   found mainly in South Island
B   on the east coast
C   the highest
D   those shown by solid black shading.

Application of ability to:

1. measure linear distance; 2. measure, estimate area; 3. work out gradient; 4. use grid reference system.

These questions refer to Ordnance Survey Map 37A (Plate II).

Question 51
Which statement is true? At Laggan there is
A   a railway viaduct
B   a post office
C   a youth hostel
D   a church with a tower

Question 52
'As the crow flies' the distance from the middle of the bridge over the River Spey at 708980 to the well at 751955 is
A $2\frac{1}{2}$ miles
B $3\frac{1}{10}$ miles
C   4 miles
D $4\frac{1}{5}$ miles.

Question 53
The area of the town of Kingussie is
A   1 sq. km.
B   less than 1 sq. km.
C   1 sq. mile
D   4 sq. km.

Question 54
Find the spot height 816 in 6594 and spot height 1951 in 6696. Assume the distance between these to be $1\frac{1}{2}$ miles. The average gradient is
A   1 in 1
B   1 in 4
C   1 in 7
D   1 in 28.

Application of principles to the explanation of generalizations

For each statement shown in the lettered column, select the most relevant explanatory principle.

Question 55
(a) The Arctic lands are sparsely populated.

    1 2 3 4 5 6 7 8

1. At higher altitudes, the rare atmosphere has diminished power to absorb heat from the sun's rays.

(b) The laterite soils of the tropics are generally poor and unproductive

    1 2 3 4 5 6 7 8

2. Water is much more conservative of heat than land.

(c)

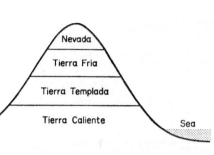

1 2 3 4 5 6 7 8

3. Exposure with respect to the midday sun makes a very considerable differerence to surface temperature.

4. Heavy rainfall rapidly removes soluble constituents.

5. Where mountains intercept rainbearing winds orographic rains result.

(d) In west-east valleys in Switzerland, settlement is commonly found on the north side.

1 2 3 4 5 6 7 8

6. Precipitation and temperature help to define the snowline.

(e) Simla and Darjeeling are healthy places for Europeans, despite their sub-tropical situations.

1 2 3 4 5 6 7 8

7. Small amounts of insolation severely limit life.

(f) The Sierra Nevada (in California) is a valuable source of water supply for irrigation of the drier lowlands.

1 2 3 4 5 6 7 8

8. Dark coloured soils and surfaces absorb more of the sun's heat than light coloured ones.

Application of theories, using a fictional and therefore novel situation

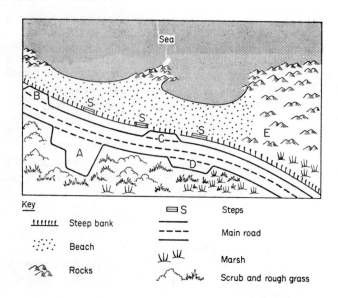

Question 56

It is a sunny July day and there are many visitors using this beach. An ice-cream and soft-drink seller arrives. Where should he park his van?

A   At (A) in the main car park
B   At (B), a roadside stopping place
C   At (C), a roadside stopping place
D   At (D), a roadside stopping place
E   At (E) on the edge of the beach.

Application of criteria based on knowledge of conventions used in sketch-map construction

Requires an *evaluation* to be made by the student.

Question 57

Look at each of these maps carefully and then decide which one is best as a *sketch* map.

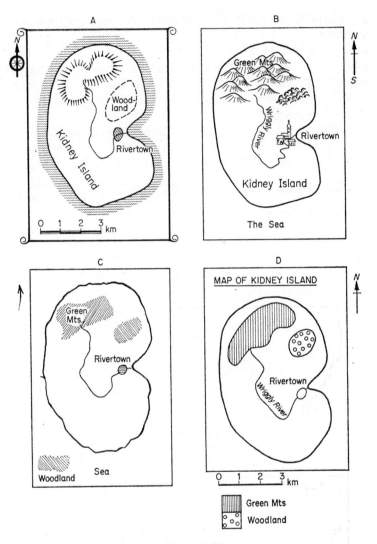

ANALYSIS

*Tests ability to recognize the way in which one element of a
geographical communication functions in relation to others*
Read this passage and study the maps.*

*Material for this item adapted from 'Changes in the Canadian Wheat
Belt 1931–69' by J. S. Dunlop in *Geography* (April, 1970).

"The first four decades of this century was a period of exploration and experimentation in the Prairies of Canada. To begin with, settlers chose land without having knowledge of its agricultural potential, and often good initial crops were obtained on land subsequently proven to be poor in nutrients. Substantial differences in soil potential were revealed as nutrients were used up and soil structure weakened.

As the true capability of land became evident many farms were abandoned and new areas opened up, e.g. 109 farm abandonments have taken place in the Lomond area (west of Medicine Hat) and, of these, 59 took place before 1931. The severe drought and economic depression, both of which began in 1929, accelerated and enlarged this process of abandonment and re-location.

Between 1931 and 1951 cultivation of wheat was withdrawn from three areas: the area between Edmonton and Medicine Hat; S.W. Saskatchewan; and S.W. Manitoba. It became concentrated into a belt occupying much of S.E. Saskatchewan, with an outlier S.W. of Medicine Hat."

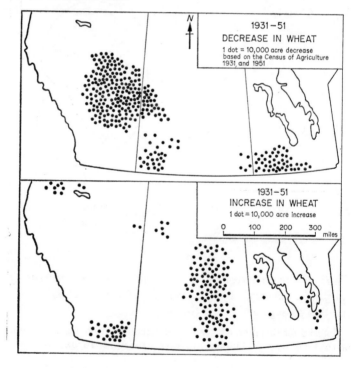

Question 58
What are the functions of the maps in this communication?
Select *two* functions.

A They present factual data in support of the text.
B They express the dynamic of wheat cultivation in symbolic terms.
C They act as a summary.
D They introduce new concepts into the study of wheat growing.
E They contradict the main sequence explained in the text.
F They offer vivid explanation to support the written thesis.
G They have no function as the central thesis has already been substantiated by the point at which the maps are introduced.

Analysis—Ability to recognize an assumption essential to a conclusion

Question 59

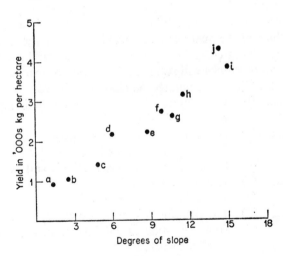

Statement of facts: The graph above shows a relationship between yield (kg per hectare) and slope (°) on a farm. Individual fields are shown as a, b, c, d, etc.

A conclusion is drawn: 'Degree of productivity depends on

steepness of slope'. Which of the following assumptions must
be made to justify that conclusion?

A   On this farm soils developed on steep slopes have a higher
    degree of fertility than soils developed in flat land.
B   On this farm all fields are fertilized as they require it.
C   On this farm the farmer works harder to make his hill
    land productive, whereas the lowland does not need so
    much attention.
D   There is a strong correlation between degree of slope and
    yield per unit area.
E   In the geography of this farm cause and effect relation-
    ships are often clearly seen.

EVALUATION

This item provides a particular end. The student is asked to determine means which will serve it best.

Question 60
A student is required to select a map or maps for use on a
cross-country route. This route will take about 12 hours.
Which of the qualities below would give him the most useful
map? Tick √ against each superior quality. Tick *ten* only.
Additional ticks will result in deducation of marks.

____(a)   It is mounted on cloth and folded.
____(b)   It is mounted and sealed on to heavy mark-
          resistant plastic.
____(c)   It is cheap and printed on paper.
____(d)   It has a well calibrated linear scale.
____(e)   Its scales are expressed verbally and as R.F.
____(f)   It has a metric scale.
____(g)   The colours are very vivid.
____(h)   The printing inks used are waterproof.
____(i)   Some phosphorescent inks have been used for
          twilight work.
____(j)   Landmarks are shown and named.
____(k)   Camping sites are shown.
____(l)   Cafes and public conveniences are shown.
____(m)   A great variety of land use is shown.
____(n)   All routes from paths to motorways are shown.

_____(o) Rights of ways and public footpaths are shown.
_____(p) Gradients are given for hills over 1:5 on main roads.
_____(q) Buildings are classed according to aesthetic and architectural merit.
_____(r) Contours are shown at 10m intervals.
_____(s) Contours are shown at 50m intervals.
_____(t) Woodland and marsh are shown.
_____(u) Hill shading is used to give a very clear pictorial effect.
_____(v) The scale used is 1:500000.
_____(w) The scale used is 1:50000.
_____(x) The scale used is 1:5000.
_____(y) The grid ref. system gives precision to 100m.
_____(z) The grid ref. system gives precision to 10m.

Such a question could be objectively marked but the qualities would require to be subjectively judged before being included or excluded from the scorer's final list.

Bibliography

BLOOM, B. S., et al. *Taxonomy of Educational Objectives*, Vols 1 and 2. Longman, 1965.

BLOOM, B. S., HASTINGS, J. THOMAS and MADAUS, G. F. *Handbook of Formative and Summative Evaluation of Student learning.* McGraw Hill, 1970.

Geography Achievement Test. National Council for Geographic Education, Canada, 1964.

GERBERICH, J. RAYMOND. *Specimen Objective Test Items.* Longman, 1956.

GOROW, F. F. *Better Classroom Testing.* Chandler, California, 1966.

GRAVES, N. J. 'School examinations', in *New Movements in the study and Teaching of Geography*, ed. N. J. Graves. Temple Smith, 1972.

——, *Geography in Secondary Education.* Geographical Association, 1971.

GREEN, J. A. *Teacher-made Tests.* Harper & Row, 1963.

GREEN, H. A., JORGENSEN, A. N. and GERBERICH, J. R. *Measurement and Evaluation in the Secondary School.* Longman, 1954, 2nd edn.

HONES, G. H. 'Objective testing in geography'. *Geography*, 1973, **58**, 29–37.

KURFMAN, D. G. 'Evaluation in Geographic Education'. Yearbook of National Council for Geographic Education, 1971.

——, 'Evaluating geographic learning', in *Focus on Geography, Key Concepts and Teaching Strategies*, ed. P. Bacon. 40th Year Book, National Council for the Social Studies, 1970.

McINTOSH, D. M. *Statistics for the Teacher.* Pergamon, 1967.

MACINTOSH, H. G. and MORRISON, R. B. *Objective Testing.* University of London Press, 1969.

MAGER, R. F. *Preparing Instructional Objectives.* Fearon, 1962.

MONK, J. J. 'Preparing tests to measure course objectives'. *Journal of Geography*, 1971, **70**, 157–62.

ROBERSON, B. S. 'Geography examinations at "O" and "A" level', *Geography*, 1971, **56**, 96–104.

ROE, P. E. 'Examining CSE Geography', *Geography*, 1971, **56**, 105–111.

SALMON, R. B. and THOMSON, G. O. B. *An Experimental Examination in Geography.* Moray House College, 1971.

Schools Council. *A Common System of Examining at 16 +* (Examinations Bulletin 23). Evans/Methuen Educational, 1971.

——, *The Certificate of Secondary Education: an Introduction to Some Techniques of Examining.* (Examinations Bulletin No. 3). HMSO, 1964.

——, *The Certificate of Secondary Education: an Introduction to Objective-type Examinations* (Examinations Bulletin No. 4). HMSO 1964.

————, *The Certificate of Secondary Education: Trial Examinations— Geography* (Examinations Bulletin No. 14). HMSO, 1966

SENATHIRAJAH, N. and WEISS, J. *Evaluation in Geography.* Ontario Institute for Studies in Education, Toronto, 1971.

GODFREY THOMSON RESEARCH UNIT, UNIVERSITY OF EDINBURGH, *An Experimental Test of Geography at Ordinary Grade of the Scottish Certificate of Education,* 1968.

VERNON, P. E. *Measurement of Abilities.* University of London Press, 1956

WOOD, R. and SKURNIK, L. S. *Item Banking.* National Foundation for Educational Research, 1969.

Index